The Last of the NUBA

by Leni Riefenstahl

Harper & Row, Publishers
New York, Evanston, San Francisco, London

to my mother

I wish to thank
members of the Sudanese Government
for their help and understanding in my work,
especially Mr Ahmed Abu Bakr,
the former Minister of Information and Tourism.
My deepest thanks however are for the Nuba—
I shall never forget
their friendship and their love.

Contents

Frontispiece
Napi had not long been married to this young girl when he died. Nuba marriage is based on love and his bride's distress is deeply and personally felt. She explained her eye paint with the words: 'Now I see Napi'.

Page 4
Among the Nuba, the Mesakin in particular tend to be self-sufficient. Many young men of the kaduma stage tend to introspection. Each will make his own lyre and will constantly play on it tunes of his own composing—sometimes rather plaintive and always individual and captivating.

Left
Generally well in control of their world, the Mesakin Nuba tend to be cheerful and friendly. Young people especially are conscious of and delight in their attractions even though they may, like Tutu, be rather shy. They are fond of ornament, decoration and jewelry and take great care with their appearance.

With the exception of the illustration on page 208 by George Rodger all the photographs in this book were taken by the author with a Leica- and Leicaflex camera on Agfacolor CT 18 color transparency film.

First U.S. Edition
Copyright © Leni Riefenstahl, 1973
© English Translation Fitzhenry and Whiteside Limited, 1974
Standard Book Number: 006-013549-2
Library of Congress Catalog Card Number: 73-4120
Printed in Italy by Arnoldo Mondadori Editore, Verona

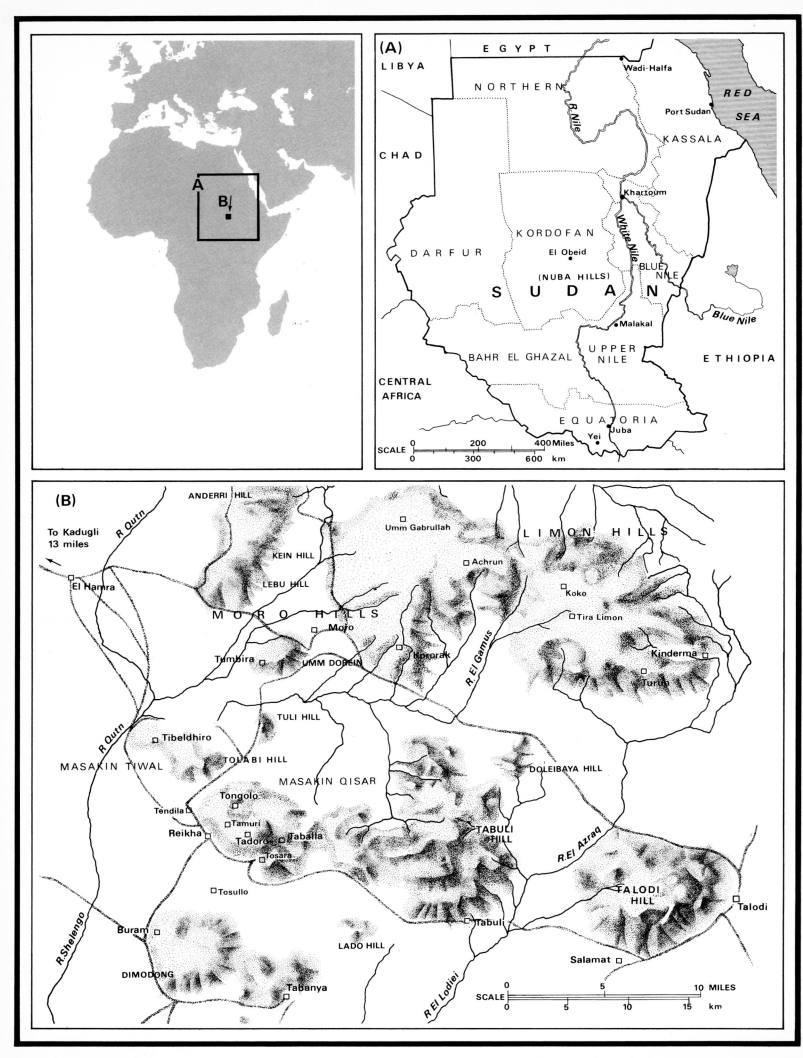

(A)

EGYPT

LIBYA

NORTHERN

CHAD

R.Nile

Wadi-Halfa

Port Sudan

RED SEA

KASSALA

Khartoum

DARFUR

KORDOFAN

White Nile

El Obeid

(NUBA HILLS)

BLUE NILE

S U D A N

Blue Nile

Malakal

BAHR EL GHAZAL

UPPER NILE

ETHIOPIA

CENTRAL AFRICA

E Q U A T O R I A

Yei

Juba

SCALE

0   200   400 Miles

0   300   600 km

(B)

ANDERRI HILL

R Qutn

To Kadugli
13 miles

Umm Gabrullah

L I M O N   H I L L S

KEIN HILL

Achrun

El Hamra

LEBU HILL

Koko

M O R O   H I L L S

Tira Limon

Moro

Kiprorak

R. El Gamus

Kinderma

Tumbira

UMM DOREIN

Turtu

TULI HILL

Tibeldhiro

MASAKIN TIWAL

TOLABI HILL

MASAKIN QISAR

DOLEIBAYA HILL

Tongolo

Tendila

Tamuri

TABULI HILL

R. El Azraq

Reikha

Tadoro

Taballa

Tosara

FALODI HILL

Tosullo

R.Shelengo

Tabuli

Talodi

Buram

LADO HILL

Salamat

DIMODONG

R El Lodiei

SCALE

0   5   10 MILES

Tabanya

0   5   10   15 km

8

How Leni Riefenstahl came to study the Mesakin Nuba of Kordofan

One sleepless night in the mid-1950s, Leni Riefenstahl began reading Hemingway's *The Green Hills of Africa*. Hemingway tells of his impressions on his first safari in East Africa; so compelling were his descriptions that Leni Riefenstahl was soon caught up by an enthusiasm that was to dominate her life from that point on. She had read the whole book through by dawn. One passage, in particular, left its mark on her: Hemingway's record in his diary of the first night he spent in his tent in Africa, of how, when he woke in the night, he would lie listening, 'homesick for Africa already'.

Whether through the power of a gifted storyteller or through the mystery of Africa itself, from that moment Leni Riefenstahl was obsessed with the desire to become acquainted with Africa. Several remarkable women have experienced the same fascination, from Mary Kingsley a century ago, to Karen Blixen, Margery Perham, Doris Lessing and Elspeth Huxley of our own day. For Leni Riefenstahl, the obsession became of such violence that it drove away all her other thoughts and attentions. With a number of friends, she sat down to write the outline of a descriptive film sited in Africa —she was then still exclusively a film-maker. It was, for her, one method of turning her desire into reality. As it turned out, within a few weeks she was able to fly with her plans for the film to East Africa, with Nairobi as her base.

Her aircraft stopped to refuel at Khartoum. She stepped out of the aircraft, dazzled by the glaring, reddish-yellow light of the dawn sun. She felt the warm movement of the air. Human figures of an intense blackness approached her out of the bright light. She was already beginning to feel the magic that the Dark Continent was to have for her.

There was an apocalyptic element in her introduction to Africa. Her intention at that time was to make a film about the persisting slave trade from eastern Africa into Greater Arabia. With this general intention, she and two companions were driving northwards from Nairobi towards the Tana River and the north-eastern district of Kenya abutting on Somalia. The skies were cloudless, the air pure. The broad savannas overwhelmed the eye. As one travels northwards, it becomes an increasingly empty and desolate area. Quite suddenly, a tiny dik-dik leapt out onto the murram road from the thorny scrub. The driver tried to avoid the animal, but as he swerved out into the deep red sand he skidded and crashed into two stones marking the edge of a bridge. The vehicle flew into the air; Leni Riefenstahl felt her head crash through the windscreen and was aware of herself and her driver dropping headlong into a waterless river bed.

It was not until several days later, after drifting back to consciousness in a Nairobi hospital, that she learned of her near-miraculous rescue. The driver had been severely injured and had lost consciousness. The African boy who had been with her had become jammed inside the vehicle.

It was a road which was used extremely rarely. Yet the victims evidently lay where they had crashed for less than two hours. As chance had it, a British District Officer, whose duty it was to inspect that particular road towards Somalia once a month, that very day crossed the bridge and saw the Land Rover lying in the river bed. He summoned help and was able to extract the injured and get them to Gorissa, 367 miles north of Nairobi. There he radioed for a small aircraft which arrived within a few hours and flew them to hospital.

Besides the injury to her head, all Leni Riefenstahl's ribs were broken and one of her lungs was damaged. The doctors were fairly despondent about her eventual recovery. She lay in hospital for several weeks thinking about the Africa she was still determined to discover. It was a dramatic baptism. Typically her obsession to become part of Africa intensified. This is how she described the impression made upon her by the sight of two Masai tribesmen within a few days of her release from hospital. 'I have paid with pain the price of initiation: now I find myself more enchanted by the African scene even than hitherto. I have fallen under its spell. Africa has been epitomized for me by two Masai warriors striding with their swinging gait beside the roadside. They wore head-dresses of black ostrich feathers, and they were carrying shields and spears. Holding themselves proudly erect, they took no notice of us at all. It was the first time I had seen Africans in their tribal dress. I could not take my eyes off these figures until they disappeared in the dust of the roadway.' Yet she was still searching in real life for what was a private inward image of the noble and primaeval African. Unapologetically romantic, unashamedly obeisant towards the beauty of the human form, she held to her own vision of an ancient and uncorrupted Africa that neither White nor Arab intruder had yet despoiled. As the months went by, she could not find the African tribe that fitted her determined preconceptions, nor did the filming enterprise work out to her satisfaction. It looked as if the perfectionist in Leni Riefenstahl was going to hold her back on the brink of another surge of creation.

And so very nearly it did.

On the last day of that prolonged visit to Africa she happened to be looking through some illustrated magazines. Her attention was drawn by a photograph of an African athlete astride the shoulders of another African. The athlete's naked body looked as if it were a statue modelled by a sculptor. The large, expressive head was set on a powerful neck. The demeanour and the pose of the African showed a sovereign self-confidence. The photographer was already well known—an Englishman named George Rodger. The illustration was captioned *A Nuba of Kordofan*.

That picture may be said to have changed Leni Riefenstahl's life. It made her do things that she would otherwise never have dreamed of doing. Her yearnings that had been directed in general towards Africa now became focused upon the Nuba. Kordofan, a province of the Sudan, at once became the centre of her plans. As she described it: 'that photograph persecuted me'. She rapidly learned from anthropologists that few Europeans had visited the Nuba, not even missionaries. These were the Nuba who live in the most southern and inaccessible valleys—not the half million or so who have become islamicized and have mixed with other peoples further north. She read all that had been written about them. Her task would be to find the Nuba and to make a pictorial record of these people that would be the work of art their beauty and magnificence demanded.

Yet it was not until six years later that Leni Riefenstahl—by then nearly sixty years old and something of a mythical figure as a film-maker before the war, half-forgotten by a nation which chose to wipe from its memory an era of its history—had the chance of turning her stubborn dream into reality. She succeeded in attaching herself to a German expedition which planned to travel through the Southern Sudan and to finish its journey in East Africa. The route of the expedition would take them through Nuer territory south and east of Malakal and due south of Khartoum. It would skirt the highlands of Kordofan, some distance to the north and west of the Nuba homeland. But it was enough for Leni Riefenstahl. If she could make her way to the central Sudan with some able bodied companions, she would somehow make an initial contact with the people that had come to fascinate her.

She left Munich on a wet and hostile day in October 1962. As subjective as ever, she felt wholly released of the greyness and the cold and the nervous stress of her home town. In Africa, a few hours after her departure, she felt at once unbound and carefree. There were all the expected problems over special permissions and passes and money. The Sudan had been independent for nearly seven years. There was the anticipated suspicion of the intentions of the travellers. Most of the district of the Kordofan had remained closed since they had come under the control of the new Sudanese Government, because of the rebellion of the pagan or christianised Negro tribes of the South against their new Arab rulers. In this upheaval the Nuba had not been themselves directly involved; but the tranquillity of the whole area had been affected. And there were other reasons for forbidding travel in the 'closed districts' without permission. Great areas of the Sudan had not been opened up by roads. The rainy season frequently rendered such roads as there were impassable with mud. In the dry season it was often difficult to find water. Such conditions meant that travellers unaccompanied by escorts were often in danger; and travellers who perish are an embarrassment to governments of emerging territories who like to represent their countries as well-serviced and controlled from end to end. And lastly there was the problem of nakedness. The Prophet Muhammad did not approve of nakedness. Western man, for his part, evidently regarded nakedness as a mark of backwardness or of guilt. That substantial members of people in the hinterland should choose to go about naked was a further source of embarrassment to governments and officials struggling to preserve an image of sophistication. And the Nuba—or, at least, sections of this Nuba—were notoriously naked.

After three weeks Leni Riefenstahl and her small group were still waiting for the end of the rainy season. While she waited she inquired about the Nuba. There was so very little that she could learn. The group whom George Rodger had photographed were of a remote and determinedly tradition-bound strand of the tribe. Even so, she had already begun to doubt the Nuba that she had seen in Rodger's photograph still survived. Rodger's expedition had taken place a decade before. She felt that perhaps she was pursuing a fantasy.

It was not so. They secured their formal permission to travel and reached El Obeid, capital of the province of Kordofan. Even there, there was no certain information that the Mesakin and Korongo Nuba still pursued their traditional way of life. Officials did not normally venture beyond Dilling. When the police chief of El Obeid saw the Rodger photograph, he said: 'I think you are ten years too late. Once you could have seen these Nuba athletes all over the Nuba hills, but now, with roads and schools built, the life of the Nuba has changed. They are wearing clothes, working on plantations and have increasingly given up their old tribal life.'

They reached Kadugli, and continued southwards in their Land Rovers on a compass bearing, forcing their way through the grasses. That part of the Nuba hills is a country of rocks and ancient trees. The bigger mountains to the south gradually drew closer, and the valley they were following narrowed as it rose. There were no people, no animals, domestic or wild, to be seen and no water. They were simply feeling their way. It was on the evening of the second day after leaving Dilling that they noticed, perched on the steep slopes of the hills ahead, a number of circular houses like birds' nests clinging to cliff tops. They had not seen such houses before. They approached closer to find somewhere to pitch camp. There on a boulder was a long-legged young girl swinging a stick, almost entirely naked, her body decorated with only a string of red beads. She turned to look at the new-comers, terrified, and with a leap disappeared into the scrub like a gazelle. They were in a region of great roots and rocks, and surrounded by a deep silence as the valley rapidly began to darken. But, before they had completed their own camp, they caught sight several hundred yards away of a group of human figures, strangely decorated. The group was led by a number of tall men, their bodies ash-white and unclothed, but wearing remarkable head-dresses. They were followed by others whose bodies were also smeared ash-white. Bringing up the rear of the procession were girls and women, also smeared with ash, and carrying on their heads calabashes and vast baskets. The travellers were indeed in the territory of the little known Mesakin Nuba.

The Africans wound up the steep slopes above the new-comers, apparently oblivious of them, clambering over scree and rocks. Then a great boulder hid them from sight. Leni Riefenstahl pursued them over the skyline. Looking down, she was presented with an astonishing spectacle. A thousand or more Africans were gathered in the light of the setting sun in an open space, ringed by trees. They were all decorated with ash, many fantastically ornamented. Hundreds of spearheads were visible among the mass of the people who had formed themselves into a number of circles of different sizes; in the centre of each of the circles pairs of wrestlers faced each other, challenging one another, locked in combat, or sometimes being carried out of the ring as victors on the shoulders of the spectators. There was an incessant drumming beneath the shrill voices of women and the shouts of the crowd. As darkness descended, the wrestling matches began to break up. Leni Riefenstahl made her way back to the rest of her party.

Thus began the saga of Leni Riefenstahl's association with the Nuba. It was to become intensely personal. While her companions continued on their main journey southwards, she remained with the Mesakin and Korongo Nuba; she was to return to them in their mountains again and again over the coming decade. Gradually she built up a pictorial and factual record which, in its devotion to the physical magnificence and primal innocence of her adopted people, will perhaps remain unique among the annals of the continent once called Dark.

Chapter one

Land & People

The Mesakin Quissayr, a Nuba tribe which, like the Korongo Nuba, has been very little exposed to the influence of civilization, live in the valleys and hills of the south-western corner of Nuba mountains in Kordofan of the Sudan. The photographs in this book were largely taken among the Mesakin, and only few among the Korongo. They were taken between 1962 and 1969. The fact that no all-season road yet leads through the region has no doubt contributed to the fact that the Mesakin still live close to nature with little contact with the outside world. No missionaries have disturbed them and very few strangers have travelled through their region. I noted that most of the Mesakin Nuba had never seen a white woman.

Their houses, resembling miniature castles, are scattered over hills which rise several hundred feet above the plain. The tallest reach 3,330 feet above sea level, with valleys running between them. By travelling thirty or thirty-five miles from Kadugli via El Hambra southwards past the Moro mountains, one reaches Reikha (in the Arabic) or Tolabe (as the Mesakin call it). The village is on the plain but this is where the hills of the Mesakin begin, and here lives the Mak, the chief of the Mesakin of Tadoro. Tadoro is the hill community of Tolabe; and it is here that I settled, choosing it as point of departure for my excursions through the entire Mesakin area.

An estimated 8,000 Mesakin Nuba still live in the fifteen to twenty various hill communities. Each larger community has its own *Mak* (chief) and its *Kudjur* (doctor and priest). The Mesakin Quissayr's neighbours are the Mesakin Tiwal. In Arabic *tiwal* means high or long; *quissayr* means short, and Mesakin, derived from the Arabic *miskin*, poor. The Mesakin are the poorest of the Nuba; but in spite of their poverty they are a happy people.

To the south live the Korongo Nuba. Because water is more plentiful in Korongo, they have more cattle and are consequently better off. They are unusually tall and strong: often a whole head taller than the Mesakin. This may be partly attributable to the fact that the Korongo, above all the men, have far more milk and *dura* (sorghum), the chief diet of the Nuba. Yet the Mesakin are opponents to be watched during the traditional wrestling ceremonies since their great agility makes up for the greater strength of the Korongo. Among the Mesakin the wrists and ankles are narrower and the hands long and well shaped. The Korongo and Mesakin cannot understand each other's language although they are such close neighbours. It is a remarkable fact that the two languages should be so profoundly different: even though these two neighbours share a common culture and are of similar origins. There are over 100 languages among the Nuba.

The Nuba live a life essentially the reverse of nomadic tribes. While the nomads live in tents which they carry with them from one source of water to another on their bullocks or camels, the Nuba live in permanent villages. The nomadic Arabs are aware of themselves as part of the wider Islamic world: the Nuba are more inward-looking, with their own religious and philosophical beliefs, and a language unintelligible to all but comparatively few in a relatively minute area. The nomads depend above all on their animals for food, Nuba primarily on agriculture. The Arab tradition is predominantly nomadic; Nuba are sedentary. This becomes clear from the way their houses are built. These houses bear witness to a remarkable culture, and to a sense of belonging to a particular place. Moreover, they are further evidence of that sense of beauty that is so much a part of Mesakin culture.

Externally, the round houses are plain and featureless. They may have evolved as small forts to defend the Nuba from slave raiders. They have survived because their structure is intimately connected with many features of family life. They never stand alone but are grouped in complexes of five or six round houses linked by connecting walls. There are no windows and the whole complex has only one entrance shaped like a keyhole. If the complex consists of five houses, the door is in one of the connecting walls, and leads directly into the inner courtyard which is covered by a flat straw roof. If there are six round houses, the door leads into one of the houses, usually the guest house through which one can reach the great inner courtyard.

These inner courts, with or without roof, are often the ornamental room of the Mesakin houses. Here the Nuba use their primitive implements to give the room a personal touch with paintings and sculpture. It came as a surprise to me to

The entrance to the granary of a Mesakin house consists solely of a round hole a little over a foot wide and about five feet off the ground. Getting in and out requires considerable agility. Folding and twisting his body the householder flicks himself in and out like an eel.

find the walls of many Mesakin houses covered in a kind of shiny blue glazing like a ceramic glaze or marble. Later I learned how the Nuba obtained this effect, which is mainly done for ornament but also probably helps the mud to resist water-erosion by hardening the surface and making it smooth. The walls were smeared with earth containing a great deal of graphite and then rubbed with the ball of the thumb for days to create this characteristic strong blue sheen. Wide borders are painted with various ornaments at the top of the mud walls. Usually it is the wall where the simple 'shower' is attached that is particularly decorated with painting and ornaments. The 'shower' is merely a calabash filled with water, usually supported on cattle horns, with a small opening at the top rim from which a thin line of water trickles down when the calabash is tipped forward by a cord.

Nuba houses are built on rock so that their bases are not destroyed by rainwater. Early travellers have reported that in the past, before British colonial power put an end to Arab slaving, Nuba houses were only built very high up in the mountains where the people felt more secure from enemies and could defend themselves better. It was difficult for British administrators effectively to bring what were regarded as the benefits of colonial rule to the Nuba population because the houses were sited so inaccessibly. So they instructed the Nuba to abandon their houses and build new ones at the foot of the mountains. The Nuba were not unnaturally reluctant to leave their houses. Whereupon, so the Nuba tell, some highland houses were burned down, which embittered the peaceful Nuba; it takes a man two years to build a Nuba housing complex since he cannot build during the five month rainy season, and he has to see to the harvest during the dry season. The administration with gradual success continues to persuade the Nuba to build their houses at the foot of the mountains, not least in order to have better control when epidemics break out.

In Tadoro, where I spent many months, I observed that the Mesakin are now building many of their new houses on the lower rocky slopes. The most difficult job here is to flatten the ground. Since the Nuba have only light working tools— an axe, a knife and a hoe—it is difficult and slow work to break up the masses of stone. Often they have to summon the assistance of friends and relatives to roll away large blocks

of rocks. Four or five men may use a tree trunk as a lever. Then they break up the large stones lying around, and wherever there is no natural rock on the ground they replace it with these small stones. The stones are put together in such a way that the water that leaks into the inner courtyards in the rainy season is drained off. Then larger stones are fetched and they are laid to form the foundation of the walls of the round huts which are built of mud. At the base, the walls are some twelve inches thick; towards the top they are thinner. They are about seven to ten feet high. At the top, wooden pegs are inset for hanging the working tools and calabashes. Once everything has been done except for the roofs, the connecting walls between the individual huts are built. The diameter of the round huts is about eleven and a half to thirteen feet, the length of the connecting walls three and a half to five feet. Finally the roofs are put on; they are made of branches or, alternatively, several millet stalks skilfully bound together with cord made from bark. For work on the straw thatch, forked tree trunks are used as ladders, and the straw is layered so skilfully that it keeps out even the heaviest rain.

Once the house is finished a celebration is held in which all the friends and relations take part and joyfully drink *marissa* beer which is brewed from fermented sorghum. This celebration takes place in the inner courtyard which usually has a roof to provide shade. By the time the builder has had his fill of *marissa*, there are more guests than the courtyard can hold and they sit on the rocks outside the house.

This inner courtyard is the central 'room' of the house It houses the cooking area, which centres on a hearth of three rounded stones on which stands a large clay pot made by the Nuba themselves. Here the social life of the Mesakin Nuba takes place. Stones or 'chairs' made from branches are used to sit on. This central court, like other rooms, has wooden and horn pegs set into the walls hung with a variety of pots, calabashes, tools and weapons all of which the Nuba make themselves and decorate with a fine sense of design. One can only enter the other round houses from the courtyard, and in two of these houses the entrance is so small that no stranger could wriggle through. The holes are usually between twelve and fourteen inches in diameter and the Nuba flick themselves through them like fish. Moreover the height at which they are located—about five feet above ground level—also makes them difficult to enter. There are various reasons for these entrance holes. They can easily be sealed off with stones or straw as is done when a house is full of *dura*. But the Nuba also use the houses with small entrance holes as bedrooms since they are protected from the strong winds. Moreover they are warmer on cool days and cooler in the heat. In addition, it is difficult for scorpions, spiders and snakes to enter. The entrances to the houses where the corn is ground and which house the huge pots for making *marissa* beer and storing water are so big that entry is easy. Their shape can vary, the openings are usually oval but none reach to the ground, and there is always a wall to climb first. Only the main entrance which looks like a large keyhole—wide and round at the top so that the women can carry their large baskets in and narrow at the bottom—reaches down to the ground.

The different houses have different functions. The man sleeps in one, the woman and small children in another. Older girls sleep in the house where the corn is ground and young boys often share their room with hens and young goats. If there are six houses in the complex, the entrance house is the guest room for visits of relatives and friends who live far away.

The hospitality of the Nuba is wonderful to experience. The most valuable offering they can make to their friends is a bowl of water and one of peanuts, of which they have very few since they can only be planted in the vicinity of the houses during the rainy season. The oily nuts are a valuable part of the Nuba's diet, but they are only eaten as a delicacy.

The family life of the Nuba is harmonious. It is noteworthy how the rank of the women is almost equal to that of the men, unlike other African tribes of my acquaintance such as the Masai, where the woman can be of less value to her husband than his favourite cow and has no freedom in the choice of husband. A Nuba girl cannot be forced by her parents to marry a particular man. Often girls who have not yet reached marriageable age are engaged to a man chosen by their parent, but they may refuse to marry the man. In such a case the dowry paid for the engagement—usually a cow, a few goats and hens—has to be returned by the girl's family.

Like most African tribes, the Nuba are polygamous. However, many Mesakin Nuba have only one or two wives, for the sexes are fairly evenly balanced in numbers and poverty can prevent many young men from paying the dowry required for a bride. Another requirement which makes it difficult for a man to marry several women is that only a woman for whom he has built a housing complex can claim to be married to him. If he wants a second wife the man has to build a second complex, which, as we have seen, is a painstaking operation. Yet I do know a fairly young Nuba man who has five wives and has built five housing complexes in a space of only seven years. He lives in Tadoro and is called Notti. No one who knows Notti is surprised. He is incredibly diligent and works from sunrise to nightfall, always remaining cheerful and willing to help. He climbs the rocks like a chamois and is quick as a weasel, and even when we used to sit together in the evening he would be plaiting cords from bark or strong grass which he either used for building his houses or as barter goods for Arab traders. In this way he managed to increase his cattle.

The more wives a Nuba man has, the richer he is and the more respected. For women are a valuable labour force, especially in the fields. They look after the household and fetch the water. Often the water holes are far away and the jugs heavy: it is astounding to see the women climb over the rocks with these heavy vessels on their heads. They take care of the small children, and, of course, prepare the food. Nuba meals are plain. There are two meals a day, at sunrise at 6 a.m. and again at sunset at 6 p.m., but the small children also get snacks in between. The diet is always the same: a sorghum gruel. Sorghum is widely cultivated in the Sudan and is a kind of millet that grows in the form of cobs on stalks up to six and a half feet high. The grains are smaller and harder than maize. They must have an extremely high nutritional value since they make up ninety per cent of the Mesakin's diet. The ripe cobs are yellow, white or reddish brown. According to the season the gruel is cooked with water or milk. There is no cow's milk during the dry season in the village, only a little goat's milk which is given to infants or pregnant women. The cows are kept far away from the villages where they graze near the shepherd's camps (*zariba*). Only the *kaduma* —the young wrestlers—drink the milk of these cows. As the idols of all Nuba tribes they need the best food and must be the healthiest and strongest of all. On rare occasions cooked beans are eaten, but these are as valuable and as rare as the peanuts, for they can be grown only near the huts where rainwater is artificially collected. Elsewhere the soil is much too dry. Since the Nuba kill their cattle only as sacrifices for death ceremonies they eat very little meat, although they are very partial to it. After the religious ceremony the meat can be eaten, but only by relatives of the deceased. Otherwise the Nuba may only eat their cattle if they die from a disease. They may also devour a goat as a rare treat a few times a year. Some Mesakin Nuba also keep small black pigs. But since there is little to feed these pigs on and they also eat human excrement, many Mesakin avoid eating their meat. Occasionally a scraggy hen is killed, and on rare celebrations there may even be roast mutton. But because of the bad pastures very few Nuba have sheep. Additional items of Mesakin diet are certain insects, field mice which they roast in the fire, the cherry-sized sour fruit of a certain tree, and the inside of the sorghum stalks.

Old people, whether male or female, are highly respected for their experience and wisdom. If an old person becomes sick or fragile he or she is looked after by members of the family. It is difficult to tell what age the Nuba reach since none of them know their age. Sometimes the stories of old people give one an idea, for instance, when old men tell of the battles they have fought against the Egyptians side by side with Sudanese soldiers. These battles took place at the end of the last century so the men must be at least in their middle or late eighties.

The Mesakin, like many related Nuba tribes, divide their life into various chronological phases. First come the children, called *nomaze*. Young unmarried girls are called *sirre*, married women *burr* and old women *kella*. Young men are *kaduma*, family fathers *urr*. A married woman is called *wariba*, a mother *ageniba*, a father *agediba*. Sisters and brothers, even half or quarter-related, are *gobbene*. The term *gobbene* can be used simply to express any degree of blood relationship.

The social structure of the Mesakin Nuba is both patrilineal and matrilineal. The family and its many branches form a clan, and the head—which can be a woman—is recognized by all the members as the authority. Among both the Mesakin Nuba and the Korongo it is usually the mother's brother who brings up the young boys. He is the 'uncle-father' who has more rights over the child than the real father. But a father does not have to part from his son if he does not want to. However, if he does, the boy will inherit from his uncle on his mother's side, rather than from his father.

The young people have a happy, free life. The children play all day under the shade of trees and are washed, fed and looked after by their older brothers and sisters. Girls of eight to twelve act as nursemaids, carrying the babies around on their hip for hours. The boys watch the cattle, lead the cows and goats to the watering places and see that none of the animals get lost or stolen by roaming nomads. The strongest boys go to the shepherds' camp while still children to be brought up by the *kaduma*, the wrestlers; this is their greatest joy.

Young girls, who are usually very pretty, lead a particularly free life. Besides fetching water they have little to do, and they enjoy this freedom before their marriage to the full. Their main interest is spending long hours decorating their bodies. While still very small, their mother or older sister pierce small holes through their nostrils and ears. The entire rim of the ears, which are later decorated with beads, are so pierced, and since all the Nuba like to be decorated, they bear the pain bravely. While the skin is still very thin when the girls are about four years old, they run about with many fine wooden pins sticking out of their ears and nose. A small hole is also bored with a thorn through the lower lip thus enlarging it more and more in the course of the years. A wire with a red bead or small ivory rod is passed through the hole as decoration. The holes in the nostrils are usually covered with red beads. They decorate themselves particularly carefully when the moonlit nights grow lighter and the *oku* dances begin.

During these nocturnal dancing festivals, which reach their height on full-moon nights, the entire youth of the village is on its feet. This is when the choice of bride often takes place. The Nuba express their love with hands and eyes. The more reticent a girl is about showing her feelings, the more chance she has of finding favour. Courtship can take weeks, or even months. For the Mesakin girls are very proud and self-assured and only become more friendly when they are quite sure they prefer one young man to all others. A girl finally shows her choice, and indicates that she is willing to meet the young man intimately when she clicks her thumb against her middle finger three times. Then the lovers disappear in the darkness, often followed by curious little children.

The dances which the Nuba call *oku* are simple round dances. The girls and youths, and even the children, lay their arms around one another's hips and dance for hours with regular stamping steps, singing all the time. A youth stands or sits in the centre of the various circles leading the choir. They improvise lyrics recording the events of the day and sing them to well-known tunes. Frequently I found that I was the subject of these songs. The Nuba love to laugh, they laugh at every clumsy movement and are quick to find humour in every sort of mildly wayward occurrence. There are never any excesses or obscenities during these festivals, but rather the love of life and joyfulness that distinguishes all the Nuba. Until they reach puberty the girls only wear a string of beads round their hips. The moment they have their first period they cover their pubic region with an apron which they make themselves from root fibres. Two kinds of fibre are used for weaving: one is called *degig*, made from the roots of the *bese* bush, (*charub* in Arabic); the other is made from the twigs of the *bahre* bush. Both types of apron are called *barega* in Nuba, *kaufus* in Arabic.

The Nuba also decorate their bodies with cicatrization. These 'beauty operations' are usually performed with sharp thorns, although fine metal knives or crystal splinters are also used. Almost every Nuba girl and man can perform the operation, but there are specialists among the Mesakin who are expert and they are rewarded for their work by presents of sesame oil or hens. Cicatrization involves some risk: piercing can cause disfigurement to the ears if it is done carelessly, and sometimes the cuts made on the body can fester. A girl's body is first decorated in this way when she has her first period, and designs are first cut on the breasts. The design varies according to taste. Ash is sprinkled onto the bleeding wounds in order to obtain a darker scar line and to raise the skin. This can produce beautiful ridges and ornaments of skin—but only if done skilfully. The upper arm and the back are decorated later. The designs cut on the back can be very beautiful and give the effect of black lace on a dark body. The abdomen is cicatrized when a girl expects her first child and a new design is added at each pregnancy.

The men also have many cicatrizations usually designed as ornaments and as a proof of courage. The greater number of beautiful designs a young man can display, the greater are his chances with the girls. According to the *Kudjur*, medicine man, cicatrization derives from a practical, medicinal purpose: it is an ancient custom among primitive people, dating back several millennia, intended to immunize the body against a number of infectious diseases just as modern vaccinations do. The wounds which were often inflamed by dust and bacteria were meant to bring out the body's powers of resistance. This explanation has a certain medical rationality. There is another factor. The operation is painful and serves to teach the Nuba to endure pain without complaint. When the Nuba are being operated upon they look into the distance as though they are quite unaffected: only an occasional twitch of the mouth betrays the great pain they feel.

Even little boys have to submit to a test of courage. When they are eight or ten years old two of their lower incisors are broken off. The Mesakin offer a medical explanation for this apparently strange custom too: their doctors say that during epileptic fits when the victim often bites his teeth so firmly together, the lack of these two teeth enables one to unclench his mouth.

Nuba girls and men remove all hair from the body and most of it from the head. This is probably for reasons of cleanliness since this area of the Nuba mountains is very dusty. Since they have very well proportioned heads, the lack of hair does not in any way disfigure their faces: on the contrary it makes them even more expressive. But they do leave a very slight growth on their head and then cut decorative patterns into this short hair with great skill and imagination, making circles, geometric shapes and small ornamental tufts. The Nuba call these hairstyles *manga*. They are further evidence of the artistic sense of the Nuba.

Among the Mesakin Nuba it is customary for young girls to withdraw into isolation for a month before their wedding. They live in a grain house where the *dura* is stored and are given particularly good and abundant food. They are only allowed to be seen by their nearest relatives and can therefore only leave their houses at night. Usually two or three girls live together. During this period their whole body is covered in white ash. Compared to this elaborate ritual of separation, the actual wedding, for which it prepares, is a relatively simple affair. There is no ceremony, and most people hardly notice it since it only takes place in a narrow family circle. In fact, the wedding does not take place at any single moment among the Mesakin but is a process spanning several stages.

Usually the girl who is to marry has already been the man's *sirre*, his girlfriend or lover, beforehand. This does not necessarily lead to marriage, for the Nuba do not consider free love before marriage dishonourable. Children born before a girl is married have the same rights and are loved and attended to in the same way as those born after. A girl who has a child but who does not marry the father, lives with her parents and can marry later.

In spite of this liberal attitude however, there are a few curious taboos connected with love and marriage. If a Nuba man falls in love with a girl and wants to marry her, and if the girl agrees, he gives a dowry to the girl's father. Close relatives on both sides are invited and *marissa* is drunk. But there are no ceremonies or rites. From now on the young girl is his wife and is described by all the Nuba as *wariba*. But since the husband has not yet built her a house, perhaps because he is still living in the *zariba* and wrestling, the wife will live with her parents until he has built it. The husband may not visit her in the daytime; if he does he has to wait in front of the door while she remains inside and they converse from a distance. Nor may the husband meet her elsewhere, not even if she already has a child by him. He may only come when everyone is asleep and he has to leave the house again in the morning 'before the cock crows'. While he is with her neither his wife nor her parents or relatives may offer him food or drink, not even if he is hungry or thirsty. Often the Nuba man has to walk many hours before reaching the house where his wife lives, so he must love her very much to make such a sacrifice. This custom, still strictly observed by the Mesakin Nuba, has an educational function: in building a housing complex the men make their main contribution to the marriage, for when it is completed the woman will take over a great portion of the heavy work. This is why the woman does not have to work for her husband until the house is built.

There are still taboos after the house is finished. The wife now lives there with him and fulfils all the duties of a wife. Yet for a whole year, although she prepares the food, she may not eat together with her husband and children. She must go to another house, usually that of relatives if her parents live too far away, and eat there. Only when the husband has confirmed that his wife is a good mother and worker is the marriage finally sealed by a small ceremony. Those present are only the very close relatives, who bring presents such as *marissa* beer, chickens or small pigs. Then the husband and wife sit down opposite each other. In front of their feet stands a pot filled with *dura* gruel and each of the two takes a spoonful of gruel in his mouth and then spits it out without swallowing it, after which they finish it together. When the ceremony is concluded they are considered to be legitimately man and wife. Now too the wife's social status is confirmed, even if the man marries a second or third wife later. Two wives never live together in one housing complex. This means that normally relations between the wives are amicable, for there is an advantage in having a husband with two or three wives. It means less work for each, since they can share it. Yet passionate jealousy can exist between women. It seldom flares between the wives, but exists when the husband has a mistress apart from his wife or wives and spends most of the nights with her. Then it can happen that a wife, armed with a stick, will beat up her husband's mistress violently and even injure her seriously. Conversely it sometimes happens that a wife will deceive her husband if he has been away for a long time. If the husband catches his rival he will beat him half to death.

Emotion runs strong among the Mesakin Nuba, and love plays an important role in their lives. Their sensitivity finds its clearest expression in their love of music. Every Nuba boy, youth and man, and almost every girl, owns a musical instrument they have made themselves; the *kaduma* usually make theirs in the *zariba*. Most of these instruments resemble a primitive lyre, but of different sizes, shapes and types. There are simple versions of the *bene-bene* as well as sophisticated ones. The sounding-board is made of a calabash cut in half, and covered with a skin with several holes burnt in it. To embellish it further, a skin is sometimes used complete with fur which is then cut into patterns. The Nuba use five strings, preferably made of steel which they buy from the Arabs in exchange for tobacco leaves or *dura*. These strings, attached to a simple round peg, can be tuned individually by loosening or tightening. Before the Nuba begin to play their lovely tunes, they often spend a long time tuning the instrument. It is interesting to note that each Nuba composes his own melodies and creates a whole repertoire. From afar I could tell by the tune who was visiting me. On waking in the morning the Nuba immediately reach for their instrument; during the siesta they often play while reclining on the ground, and in the evening their tunes sound from the cliffs where they sit in front of their houses; they sound all around the neighbourhood for the Nuba even play their inimitable melodies while walking.

Although the Nuba had to fight hard in the past to defend themselves against slave-hunters, they are peace-loving people. Robbery and murder are despised and rarely occur except for the traditional goat-stealing. However, there is one exception. The introduction of money has had a negative influence on their character, and this was sadly apparent to me during my last expedition in 1969. During my early visits my crates could be left in the open, unlocked, for months, but now this was no longer possible. This change is explained by the fact that, because of a very poor harvest, some of the Nuba tribes had to go to the towns to earn some money to buy cattle or a few goats. In the towns they saw how everything could be bought with money and this had a destructive effect on them. Until then, cut off from the outside world, they had made everything they needed for themselves except bits of iron for their implements (the Mesakin have no iron nor smiths), the white cloth in which they wrap their dead, and the colourful fabrics with which the wrestlers adorn themselves—all of which they obtained by barter from the Arabs. They knew nothing else and were happy and content with this life. The possession of money used to be foreign to them. But soon the inevitable march of civilization will reach the Mesakin Nuba and change them too. I was fortunate to get to know them whilst their traditional way of life still existed, and to be able to fix this in pictures, films and recordings. It was a view into a Paradise that will soon vanish.

The Mesakin do not have a single chief of the whole tribe. An imprecise notion exists that 'sovereignty' rests with the whole people. Each of the Mesakin Nuba's hill communities has a Mak and a Kudjur. The Mak (Mak—Arabic for chief) is the leader, responsible for justice and settling social problems. At the same time he is the authority, recognized by the government, who tries to reconcile the interests of the Nuba and of the Arabs. His position is hereditary, like that of the Kudjur who acts as priest for religious and cult matters and who is far more revered by the Nuba. Legal proceedings take place once a week before the house of the Mak, and the chiefs of other hill communities may also take part. Early in the morning the chiefs assemble in the shade of old baobab trees. They are joined by the bareda, the most repected men in the various communities (what we might call a council of elders), and then the alleged offenders appear and judgment is given after long deliberations.

The accused submit to this court quite voluntarily. They are accompanied by close relatives who stand just outside the circle, which the accused enters when his name is called. Sometimes the accused is one individual, but there can be two or more 'charged' together. The accused sit on the ground, their legs outstretched and eyes cast down as though conscious of guilt. Then the Mak questions them calmly. The accusations are almost always the same and the accused generally know the sentence in advance. There are three main offences. Firstly, adultery and 'stealing a sirre' (young girl); secondly the traditional theft of goats; and thirdly inheritance questions. Adultery is punished severely. If the accused is a man he has that very day to pay to the deceived husband the equivalent of the dowry the husband paid to his wife's family (one or two cows) and, according to the gravity of the case, he goes to prison for between three and six months. The theft of goats is committed almost exclusively by very young wrestlers while living in the zariba. After such a theft they arrange a goat dinner to which they also invite their companions. Even young men who only took part in the meal are given the same prison term as the actual wrongdoer.

The Mak has two or three Nuba 'policemen' to call upon who conduct the offender on the thirty-five mile walk to Kadugli there he is handed over to the Sudanese police and is imprisoned. These Nuba policemen have never been attacked by the prisoner although the Nuba men are much stronger than their guards. Only once did an accused Nuba wrestler not appear before the court and flee to Khartoum. But he fled only because he considered himself innocent: he had arrived at the goat dinner late and had allegedly only received a gnawed bone! He considered three months of prison too severe a penalty for this, so he disappeared over the hills. He was Tukami, one of the best wrestlers of Tadoro and a good friend of mine. After a year he returned to Tadoro to pay off his penalty with money he had earned by working hard in Khartoum. Unlike other Nuba men he had not liked it in town and was glad to return to his usual way of life. In prison the Nuba are employed as road workers and in agriculture, and when they return they are welcomed like heroes.

As for 'stealing a girl', we have already noted that free love is permitted among the Nuba. But there are certain laws. For instance, if a young girl is engaged, that is if a dowry has been paid for her and she has been promised to a man whether by her own wish or that of her parents, no other man may sleep with her. If he does and the *Mak* is told, the man goes to prison. If the lack of faith is clearly the fault of the girl, the girl is punished by being sent to prison in the same way. Free love is only allowed if both partners are free and are not therefore infringing someone else's rights.

There are other taboos among the Mesakin that are punished not by imprisonment but with contempt, and this they consider far more severe. One such taboo is that no Mesakin Nuba may have sexual intercourse with his wife while she is pregnant. This is one reason why pregnant women move into their parents' house. If the husband should nevertheless secretly visit his wife one night and be discovered, he can no longer show his face in the village. Even the children would point at him and scoff. His only recourse is to move to another Nuba village. Up to two years after the birth the woman still does not have sexual intercourse since she nurses the infant for this period. According to the Nuba belief, sexual union during the period when human life is being created would make the child unclean and the parents would be punished for it later by the child catching a disease. For fear of this the Mesakin still observe their traditional law.

The Nuba are great lovers of children. Unfortunately infant mortality up to the age of three is very high: almost 50 per cent. This is caused mainly by water-borne diseases. Moreover the Mesakin Nuba are still too shy to bring their sick children to a hospital. The Sudanese government has set up small dispensaries even in the most remote Nuba valleys, supervised by a medical assistant and equipped with bandages and the basic medicines, all free. But the same problem arises among the Mesakin as Albert Schweitzer had to face among the Fang and Bakale: he had to spend years winning the confidence of the inhabitants before he could help them. The family does not want to be separated from the sick member and relies on the powers of the *Kudjur*.

In the past the position of the *Kudjur* must have been extremely important. He was the rain-maker and on him was thought to depend whether the harvest was good or bad; he had power over life and death and lost his own life if he failed. Today he has a lower status. He is still a priest and doctor and adviser to many, but he assumes his most important role only when the Nuba want to make contact with the souls of the deceased. I have witnessed one such spiritualist session in Tadoro. In such a session the *Kudjur* is shut in the house of the deceased. Using a hen as a medium, he tries to establish contact between the dead soul and members of the family. If this contact succeeds, which is not always the case, the members of the family seated outside the closed house question the deceased and, as they firmly believe, receive their answers through the actions of the hen as interpreted by the *Kudjur*, whose voice they hear through the narrow entrance of the house.

**Captions for pictures
on pages 25 to 72**

25
The only door in a Mesakin house-compound which reaches all the way to the ground is the main entrance. The wide top allows women with bulky loads to pass through easily.

26–27
In the village of Tutholo, on the opposite side of the valley to Tadoro, houses are built in groups of five or six like miniature castles. The small fields nearby are used for growing crops which need constant watering, like beans or peanuts. The baobab tree is useful since it grows where water is scarce. Its bark can be used for rope and the pith of its seed-pod is edible.

29
Mesakin houses used to be built high up in the hills for protection. Nowadays they are usually built lower down the slopes, so that people do not have so far to walk to the fields. The rocky terrain makes it hard work to clear a plot for building, but provides convenient stones for foundations.

30 above
These strange, craggy hills are near Dilling, north of Kadugli.

30 below
Groups of houses at Tabala in the shade of another baobab tree. Small patches of ground are cleared near the houses for cultivating tobacco. The Nuba are passionately fond of tobacco which they consume as snuff, but they exchange much of their crop for salt, pearls and gaily coloured cloth. Peanuts and beans, which also need constant watering, are similarly grown near the houses.

31
This picture shows the considerable height of some Nuba houses. The outer walls are about six and a half to ten feet high, and the rooms are ten to sixteen and a half feet high in the middle.

32
Opening to the 'corn house' blocked with straw. The crop of dura is stored there. The 'master of the house' sits proudly in front of his own property.

33 above
Nuba taking a mid-day rest because of the great heat in the shade of a rakoba, which is to be found next to most of the Nuba houses. The rakoba—the word comes from Arabic—is a shelter with a covering of dura stalks supported by slender tree-stems.

33 below
It is the duty of the young men to look after the cattle. The pride of the Nuba is their cattle. Indeed cows represent property, and determine social standing. A man with five or more is well off.

34
Not only the young men are addicted to the music of the lyre. A young girl here sits outside a house playing a variety of the same instrument which uses as a sounding-box a semi-spherical gourd inverted on the ground.

35
Meat is a comparatively rare luxury for the Nuba. Game is hunted but is hard to find, and even a long expedition rarely produces more than the occasional rabbit. Small domestic animals are not plentiful and cattle are normally killed only for funerals. But when a cow is sick and is anyway likely to die, it is killed and eaten: one such is here being cut up.

36
Curious girls looking into the hut which the Nuba built for me. Because of their vivacious miming and unsuspicious nature I gradually began to pick up their language. They have delightful names like Kaka, Kiki, Notto, Nolli and Tutu.

37 above
Old people spend more of their time at home. They often care for their grandchildren while the parents are at work. Their experience is valued by their children: they are consulted whenever circumstances are difficult and particularly when danger threatens.

37 below
A sick girl from Tadoro is tended by the Kudjur, the medicine man—in whom his people have profound confidence. He is rewarded by a chicken, marissa or even a goat.

38 above
The Mesakin work very hard for most of the time, but they never lose the knack of total relaxation. An entrance to one of the rooms in a compound can be a good perch to while away a few moments with a song on one's lyre.

38 below
Blue graphite is rubbed into the surface of the mud walls of houses as an ornament and as a protection. Small calves may be kept in the 'granary' house if they need special care, as the small entrance keeps the inside cool in the heat and warm at night.

39
One corner of the compound is devoted to a 'shower'. A gourd containing water is supported on pegs stuck in the wall, so that a steady stream will pour out as it is pulled forward by the person bathing. The stones of the floor are arranged so as to allow the water to soak away.

40 above
The same care and skill which goes to construct a house is devoted to its decoration. Natural earth colours— ochres and reds mainly—are supplemented by white from lime and black from soot or charcoal. Decoration is mostly in abstract geometric patterns, but direct representation is also used.

40 below
The Nuba are not aggressive, but efficient self-defence was necessary for survival. Weapons are prized possessions: they are made with great care and are handed down as valuable heirlooms. Shields made of elephant or rhinoceros hide are often beautifully decorated, and are still used in funerary spear-fights to honour the dead.

40 centre
Sometimes in the decoration of houses there are representational figures which are hard to identify precisely. But in appearance, style and technique they have parallels throughout Africa from the Tassili frescoes to Bushman paintings. They are possibly therefore inherited from the cultures of the earliest inhabitants of the continent.

41
In many Nuba huts one can see stylised representations of the female breast. Anthropologists believe this indicates that in the remote past the Nuba had a matriarchal society. A further indication of this is to be found in the respect they show their mothers, wives and sweethearts.

42
Decoration by cicatrization is common to most of the hill peoples of the Sudan. After the initial cut has drawn a little blood, Goggogorende here outlines with it the design of an animal which he wishes his friend to cut on his chest. The beads and brass bracelets are also traditional adornments of the Mesakin.

43 above
Following the line which his friend has drawn, Nalu cuts firmly into Goggogorende's skin with a sharp bamboo knife. The operation is not only a means to produce a decoration, but also a process by which the young men learn to bear pain with fortitude. To have a number of such cicatrizations is to show that one is a man.

43 below left
Once the cutting of the design is complete, the edges of the skin may be lifted with a thorn or tweezers, and earth, or preferably ash or charcoal, rubbed into the wound to ensure that it heals with a properly raised scar. The result ideally should be a sharp and well-defined welt in the pattern desired.

43 below right
The 'model' for the design which Goggogorende chose was Gumeri, whose cicatrization is a good example of how a design should turn out, and who represents, it is hoped, what the marking will look like when it has healed. The dots on the shoulders are also characteristic of Mesakin.

The Last of the Nuba

44 above

There were Christian Kingdoms on the Nile to the north of the Nuba Hills from the sixth to the fifteenth centuries. It is tempting to see a Christian survival in designs like this, although any actual historical connection has yet to be proved between this part of the Nuba Mountains and Christian Nubia.

44 below

If the operation of cicatrization is not done with great care and skill a scar can heal unevenly. This design is clear enough, but it has not come out quite as precisely as it should—in places it has, as it were, 'run'.

45

This very precise cross design has been repeated on each breast, on the shoulders, and lower down on the arm, making for an effect of considerable elegance and also making this young man the envy of his friends. His ear-lobes are also pierced and he wears a traditional necklace.

46

A girl undergoes cicatrization first at the onset of menstruation when a design, usually consisting of lines of little dots, is cut on the upper part of her chest and breasts. On her first pregnancy the abdomen is cut with a similar design, and at each successive pregnancy further designs are incised.

47

Young men, if they are friends from the same cattle camp, or if they are members of the same family, will often adopt the same style of decoration to complement and compliment each other. They will perform the operation each on each. Both here have the wings of their noses pierced to take a silver ring.

48–49

A favourite form of decoration, and one in which great individuality is possible, is cutting designs, called manga, in the hair. Mazes like this, straight lines, isolated clumps or plaits of hair arranged in rows— the variations are endless and a good design will be much admired and sometimes copied.

49

A young girl's ears are pierced very early when it is thought they are still 'soft'. The holes are kept open with thorns or small sticks, and eventually silver or copper rings will be inserted. This girl has an unusually large number of these sticks.

50

Girls in their teens devote a lot of time to decorating themselves. Bead ornaments, provided that they are of the right colour, are a great favourite for special occasions, for example when going to watch a wrestling match.

51

Toddo—her name means 'Bead' or 'Jewel'.

52

Although too young yet to have to undergo cicatrization, this girl already has a full complement of ear-rings as well as a nose-ring.

53

Nolly, a young girl of Tadoro.

54–55

In addition to cicatrization a girl will enhance her beauty by oiling her skin until it shines. She uses valuable and expensive oil pressed from peanuts or sesame seeds. She will probably also pierce the rim of her ears, her nose and her lower lip to support additional pieces of finery.

56

The Mesakin will make jewelry not only from 'imported' materials like metals and beads, but also from a wide variety of local and natural products—animal skins, grass or palm-fronds for bracelets and anklets, leather for belts (now also 'imported') and collars. A variety of seeds are used as beads—'Job's Tears' or neem-tree seeds being most common.

57

Tukami is a famous wrestler— champion of his village and its chief representative in inter-village contests, renowned for his strength and bravery. He is also an expert player on the bene-bene, and has here a particularly fine instrument which, of course, he has made himself.

58

Older men, even when they have families, are reluctant to cut themselves off from the life of the kaduma, the wrestlers in the cattle camp.

59

This girl's elaborate cicatrization pattern has 'run' a little in places— perhaps the cuts were made too close to each other, or maybe in rubbing in the ash they became infected. But this does little to reduce her obvious charm.

61

This young mother with her child came to visit the author in her shelter. She has prepared her hair with particular care. White crosses on her abdomen indicate that she is menstruating and may not therefore pursue her normal household tasks and cannot be touched.

62–63

A married couple of the Masakin tribe from Dormo. It is very rare to see men and young girls together. It is normal for young men to go hand-in-hand, but girls and youths usually walk about in separate groups. It is only at their Oku festivals that they can be seen dancing and playing together.

64–65

The end of the dry season is extremely hot—grass is tinder-dry and can catch fire, as it has here, spontaneously. Only around compounds in the hills is the grass burnt deliberately and under supervision to prevent casual fire from catching the thatched roofs of the houses.

66–67

A kaduma from the Korongo Hills, with his brothers and sisters. In the past this kind of belt was worn by all Masakin and Korongo Nuba, but nowadays it is seldom seen. The belt is made from a branch which is bent over the heat of a fire. The spherical object attached to it is made from clay and beeswax. The Nuba call this belt a dindi.

69

A girl from Fama in the Korongo Hills. For an important wrestling match the girls dress up for the honour of the village no less than to impress their own young men. She has oiled her skin, elaborately dressed her hair and put on her choicest pieces of jewelry.

70–71

Gua, like Tukami, is renowned as a wrestler. He is champion of his village and the victor of many fights. He will also help to train the younger wrestlers so that they will be successful in their turn.

72

A girl, specially decorated for an important tournament, carries a gourd on her head as she travels to the match. The spectators will drink beer, but the wrestlers themselves only water.

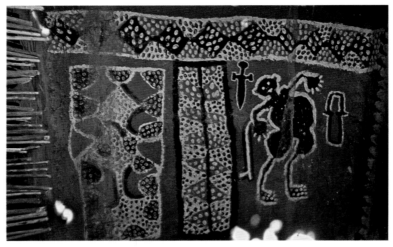

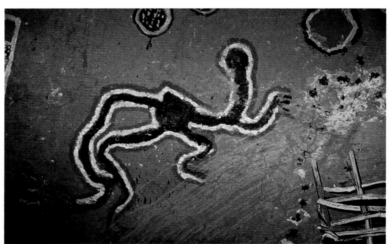

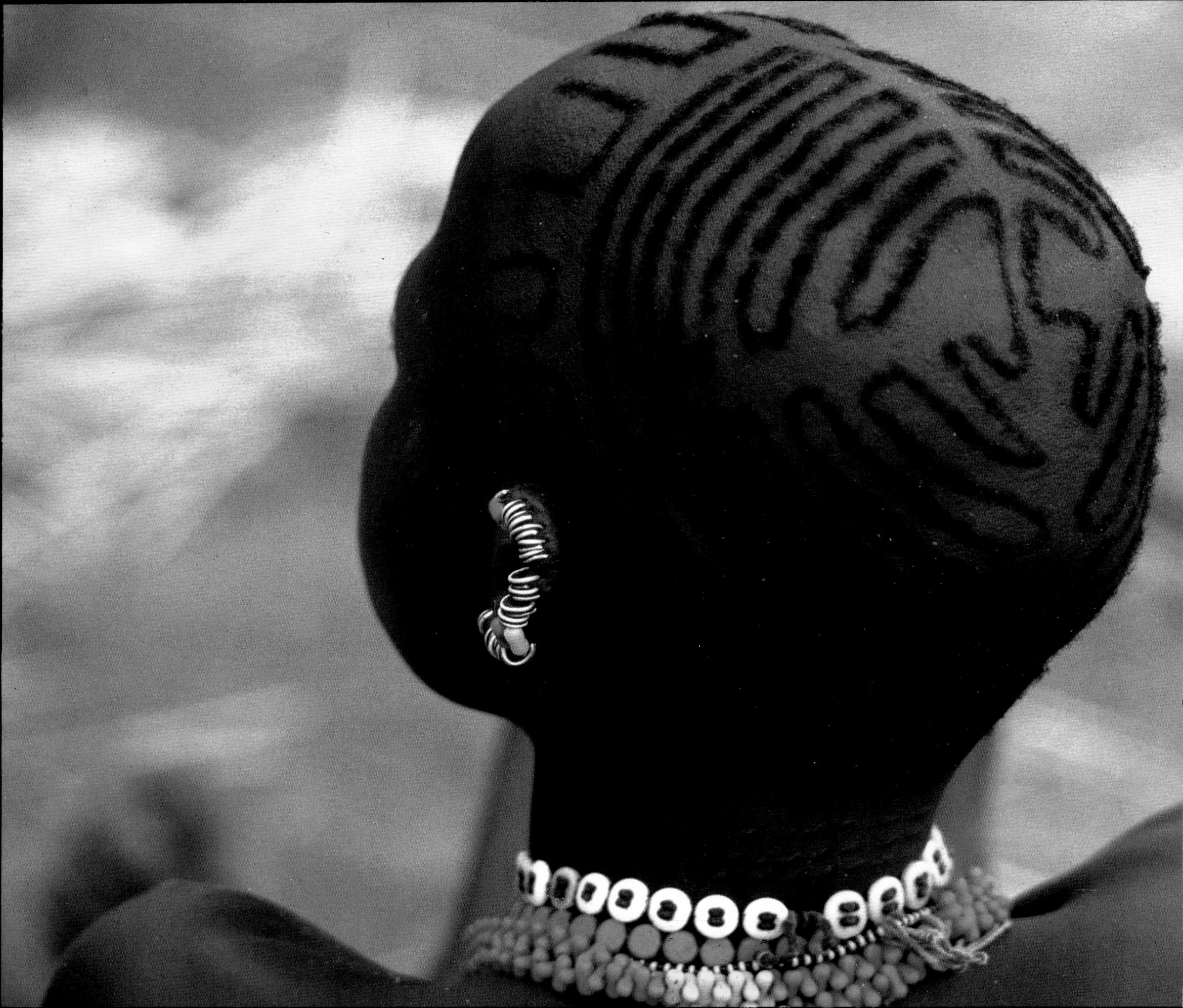

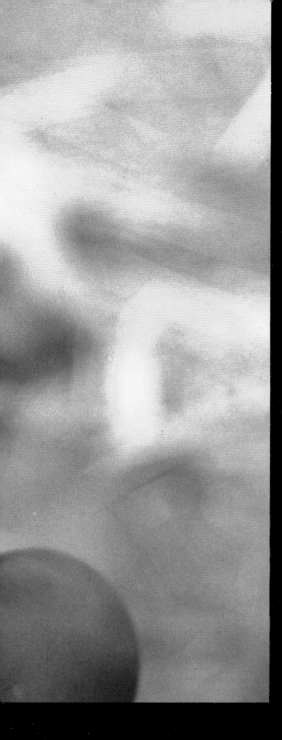

Chapter two

Harvest

Harvesting in Mesakin is a communal activity. Each man in turn will call the other men of the village to help him with the corn he and his wife have grown on their fields. His wife will make millet beer with which everyone will be entertained, strengthened, and rewarded for his labour.

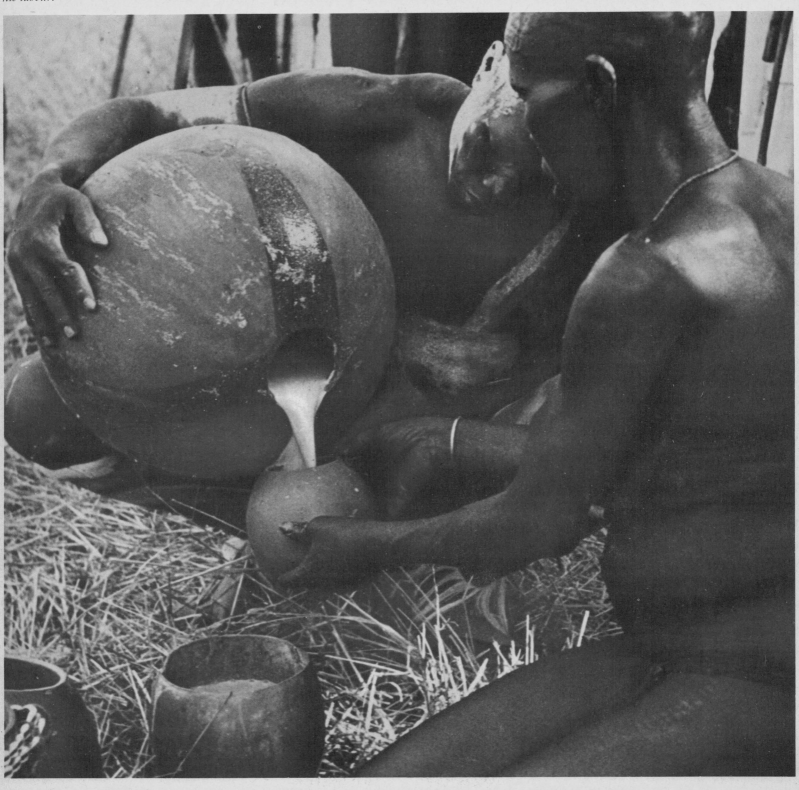

The Nuba are an agrarian people rather than cattle-breeders. For the description of the nutrition and harvesting of the Mesakin Nuba tribe I have drawn freely upon the results of scientific research carried out by Rolf Engel in 1962–63 among the Mesakin Nuba for the Max-Planck Institute, which he published in his *Spezielle Untersuchungen der Landwirtschaft in den Nubabergen* (Special Research on Agriculture in the Nuba Mountains). I was with him every day while he was carrying out his research among the Nuba, and during my own later expeditions I have observed that the findings of Rolf Engel still hold good.

It is worth noting that the Mesakin themselves produce virtually everything they need for their survival. They therefore enjoy a fundamental independence, although this does not mean to say that they have an abundance of the necessities of life. This they have only in good harvest years. After less good harvests they have to endure many sacrifices and in bad harvest years quite a number of Nuba actually die. Hunger can be the Nuba's greatest enemy. Since they seldom have money and have few goods for barter they can buy neither grain nor cattle in times of famine. I would ask my Nuba friends how they survived these times of need and they all gave the same answer. With a melancholy smile they would say: '*Nuba pengo*' (Nuba die). They look upon death as simply a matter of fate—which they do not resist or struggle against. It is almost incomprehensible that during good harvest years the Mesakin should not stock up for bad years. If they have a large excess of *dura* (sorghum vulgare) in a good year they hold tribal and family feasts until this excess has been used up. Since a good harvest is vital to the Nuba it is easy to understand the high position of the *Kudjur* priest. In the past the *Kudjur* must have had great importance and power, which is now diminishing more and more. Nevertheless, some of the cult usages connected with the harvest still survive. For instance many of the Mesakin Nuba live very continently before the harvest is brought in, because according to their religious beliefs sexual intercourse would exert an unlucky influence on the harvest. Moreover they dust themselves with white ash during some of the harvest work, though this applies almost exclusively to the men. The women are

A slightly longer break occurs in early September, if the hoeing was finished on time because the rainfall was not too heavy. At this time the quick-ripening dura *in the fields near the houses are harvested for immediate consumption according to need. Some Nuba use this period in order to make new land arable for the coming year. The* dura *has to be hoed a fourth time in some fields particularly on areas of virgin land or after heavy rainfalls. Then the sesame is ripe.*

October is still taken up with the sesame harvest. And at the end of the months the first peanuts are dug up.

In early November the men have less to do on the fields and only go out every second or third day. In the second half of November there is more activity again. The peanut and sesame harvest must be finished. Drying places have to be prepared for the heavy dura, *beans have to be picked and perhaps also cotton.*

In early December, the heavy dura *is cut. The men do the cutting, women gather the* dura *heads and put them in their baskets. On average, each year every woman carries on her head one to three tons for some three to five miles from the outer-fields to the drying grounds—the latter are fenced in with high thorny hedges as protection against animals.*

This concludes the work outside in the fields for some time. Now the stalks are chopped off, and if necessary the tobacco leaves are picked and prepared. A great number of tribal ceremonies take place during this period. Almost every day the whole village walks distances of up to twenty-five miles to attend their traditional tribal wrestling matches. Furthermore the huts are repaired, new ones constructed and dry firewood is gathered. The women thresh small amounts of dura *and grind it into flour for the daily food.*

Finally, in March, the dura *is taken from the storage places near the village to threshing grounds, usually it is threshed communally by the men with simple, 32 inch-long wooden pestles, cleaned by the women and carried home. It takes a whole month till everything has been threshed and stored.'*

The very sandy soil of the threshing places is specially prepared by the women who mix cow dung with water to make a mash which they distribute evenly on the ground by hand. Very soon, the area spread in this fashion becomes stone hard in the burning sun, and as the first rain falls at the end of April the cycle begins again.

Concerning the organization of the work Engel writes:

'The normal labour force in Nuba families consists of the man and his wives. Group work is a constant arrangement here. It is made up of family groups of neighbours, friends and occasional guests. Marissa beer (made from dura) *is the only reward given in group work. So the organization of group work requires a certain capital outlay in the form of* dura. *But the good fellowship during and after the work is as important as the beer.'*

On food consumption Engel says:

'In all the families the daily diet was dura *gruel. This gruel was cooked in the evening by the woman for the next day and divided up into individual portions. The quantity of pure* dura *consumed per head per day was measured at seventeen to thirty ounces and usually persons working full-time consumed twenty-one ounces.*

Besides the main diet of dura, *sauces were eaten with it made from sesame and beans spiced with dried leaves from the trees. Moreover large quantities of* marissa *beer were drunk. Five to eight pints or more per person per day were not unusual. . . .*

Women and children were not excluded from enjoying the marissa *beer either. Especially during the dry season when the supply of vitamins was lowest, the millet beer has its legitimate place.*

Peanuts were eaten raw or roasted. They served mainly for feeding the children. . . .'

It is rare for the Nuba to be able to enrich the low-protein diet with animal meat, for there is very little game in the Mesakin territory because of the shortage of water in the seven dry months. Also, very few Nuba have guns that shoot. Most of those they have are old inherited rifles for which they now have no ammunition and which can no longer be repaired. They are kept mainly as 'trophies' of their ancestors. If however, a Nuba has a rifle that still shoots he uses it for firing salutes during wrestling matches and funeral ceremonies. To find an Arab gunsmith who can make them cartridges that fit these ancient pieces, they often have to walk more than sixty miles. For reasons of economy they use the cartridge cases several times—and the bullets too, which they extract from the animal again and again. Very rarely they hunt young gazelles, sometimes wild rabbits, but their most common prey is birds. Occasionally the Nuba assemble for the hunt equipped with little more than sticks. The outcome is usually meagre. Yet the Nuba are happy even if they bring home only a thin little rabbit after running around in the burning sun for more than ten hours. Older men who also take part in these hunts often collapse, and it is no rarity for a Nuba to pay for this excessive effort with his life.

The only animal feared by the Nuba is a variety of cat which could be the serval or, possibly, the leopard. It has the reputation of stalking among the rocks and is seldom seen in the plain. Some Nuba wear the spotted pelt as loin cloths. The only other wild animals are monkeys—the reddish brown rhesus—but they have also become rare. The Nuba consider them a delicacy. They also consider fish a great delicacy. These are only to be found in small numbers during the rainy season at remote watering places.

Rolf Engel writes:

'During the period of research no consumption of animal protein could be noticed since they only slaughter their own cattle on special occasions.

The diet of the Nuba cannot remotely be described as having full or even sufficient nutritional value. In the main working period (hoeing, carrying), an energy balance is not achieved. Work observations and pulse counts during the period of heavy work have been estimated at over 3000 KCAL. But besides calories the major danger points are the generally poor provision of vitamins and the frequently minimal consumption of animal protein.'

These facts make it even more surprising that Nuba men have an athletic build rare in any other African tribe.

The Last of the Nuba
Captions for pictures
on pages 81 to 96

81

Fields of tobacco require special preparation: the clay is broken up into separate holes, each of which will take a single plant. This traditional—and immensely ancient— implement is a form of shovel being used here by a young wrestler.

82–83

The whole family—a man's wives, his children and sometimes his friends—will help him with his tobacco fields for the crop is an important and valuable one. It is hard work to prepare the ground, and once the tobacco is planted it must be watered constantly if it is to survive. The individual holes are designed to concentrate the water around each plant.

84–85

Water is always a problem in this part of the Sudan. In the dry season holes often must be dug deep to find any water at all, it is then handed out in pots and calabashes. Sometimes several men must form a chain up the side of the pit, or even stand on each others' shoulders if the well is narrow, in order to reach the surface.

86

Water for cattle is hauled up from a well by boys, and it is then poured into a shallow clay pan from which the cows can easily drink. The clay of the trough must be repaired constantly. The water is poured through a bunch of leaves in order to strain out any rubbish which may have fallen into it.

87 above

Digging a water hole involves considerable labour. Much of the work has to be repeated each year at the beginning of the dry season, as the rains fill in the holes. The clay mud is broken up with a hoe and then scooped up and thrown out of the hole by hand.

87 below

Surface water is plentiful in the rainy season—indeed, too plentiful for ease of transport. Much of the plain around the Nuba hills consists of clay soil which retains the water for some time. The Government is experimenting with scooping out large reservoirs which will retain water from the rains throughout the dry season.

88

Most of the heavy work in the fields, especially the initial clearing, is done by the men, but the women do all the lighter work. They help with the planting and they do the weeding while the millet is growing. At the time of the harvest their job is mainly to transport the heads of grain, first from the field to the drying stack nearby, and later from the stack to the village.

89

The dried-out heads of the corn are carried by the women in baskets of local manufacture. The gourds are for water.

90–91

The heaviest work done by the women is carrying the harvested grain from the collection points to their houses, which are often situated high up in the hills on steep rocky slopes. The women make this journey twice a day, carrying their heavy burdens of seventy to eighty pounds a distance of three to four miles and sometimes more. It is remarkable that they do not seem to find the work at all strenuous and remain cheerful and contented.

92

After the initial threshing, the pieces of stalk and the cobs are removed from the pile of millet on the threshing patch by raking with a two-pronged fork. Anything the men do in connection with the harvest is a sacred activity concerned with the fertility of the crops, and hence of the people as a whole: ash is worn as a symbol of this and as a blessing on the work.

93 below

When the millet stalks have been cut from the stalks they are left on racks near to the fields to dry out, so that they are less heavy for the women to carry up to the village. The stalks are also useful for building houses, shelters and fences in the village— especially so as wood for these purposes is hard to find. They have been tied in bundles and will be carried up later by the men.

93 above

Once the larger pieces of stalk and cob have been removed from the millet heads by the first threshing, the smaller bits and the husks are removed by beating with wooden implements like cricket bats. This operation takes place near the village on a piece of ground whose surface has been specially prepared with a mixture of mud and dung. When dry this produces a hard flat surface.

94–95

The men, covered for this important occasion in ash, together carry out the first stage of threshing by beating the millet heads with an implement like a polo-stick. This breaks up the heads and enables the larger bits of stalk and cob to be raked out.

96

After the threshing, each woman stores her grain in the special granary hut in her compound. She takes it out as it is needed and grinds it in another hut where the lower grind-stone is set into a mud 'table'. From the flour she prepares a stiff porridge which constitutes a very high proportion of the Nuba diet.

Chapter three

Zariba

Pages 98–99
For Nuba men, the best period of their life is that which, as young kaduma, they spend in the cattle camp. The boys take the animals out to find water and grazing, and the young wrestlers practise for forthcoming contests. They eat twice a day as the sun rises and sets.

A wrestler from the Zariba.

The *zariba*, a herdsmen's and wrestler's camp, which the Mesakin call *noppo*, usually lies on the plain several miles from the villages. It is hardly visible, hidden as it is by high grass and shrubs. It is a round area fenced in by a thorn hedge and always has a shade-giving tree in the centre. When dusk falls the herdsmen drive the cattle into the kraal where they spend the night in shelter. The Nuba build small clay huts for the young calves. The herdsmen and wrestlers, called *kaduma*, sleep in the open when they live in the *zariba*.

From the outside, the Nuba herdsmen's camps look little different from those of other tribes. But if, as I did, one spends several days and nights in a *zariba* it becomes clear how great an importance all the Mesakin attach to it. It occupies a key position in their life and it is only here that one can approach the ideas and religious beliefs that shape the life and character of the Nuba. No female may normally set foot in a *zariba*, not even mothers. The fact I was allowed to stay there was because as a 'white' woman I was, in certain respects, exempt from internal Nuba sanctions.

Every young Mesakin boy longs to live in the *zariba*. It is the school through which almost all the Nuba men pass. By the age of thirteen every youth will have gone to live in the *zariba* provided he is healthy. For a young child to be accepted is an honour. Only children of character and intelligence are entrusted with looking after the cattle. Moreover, these boys must show signs of becoming good wrestlers. Wrestling is the fundamental expression of the Nuba view of their world. From the moment when, as a child, he can just about stand up, success in wrestling will be the main aspiration of a man's life. His fellows will bid farewell to his spirit with a wrestling match on the anniversary of his death. Without the *zariba* there would be no wrestling matches.

The cult customs of the Nuba have also survived in very marked form in the *zariba*. Above all there is the implacable law that a youth or man who lives in the *zariba* may not sleep with a girl. The Nuba firmly believe that sexual intercourse at this time would weaken them. So they submit willingly and even proudly to this traditional custom. In order to show externally too that they are *zariba* dwellers, they cover themselves with white ash (*weega*) or paint ornaments on their body with a mixture of ash and milk beaten into cream. A Nuba who sleeps with a woman will never have ash on his body. Ash is the key to the sacred. It is produced by burning wood—wood from a tree which once grew strong and tough. Ash, essence of the tree, is the essence of growth and strength and ultimately of life itself. Clothing oneself with ash, for the Nuba, is to take on strength and a certain holiness. The wearing of ash reveals wrestling as an essentially religious event. In the center of each *zariba* lies a great heap of this white ash which every Nuba rubs onto his body in the morning after washing. The forms of the ornaments they paint on their body with the ash are improvised individually and have no cult significance.

Before the first sun rays hit the *zariba* the Nuba are busy. Some of them milk the cows. Each cow scarcely produces half a pint of milk, owing to the dry grass. A boy fetches the wood for the fire and watches the pot in which the *dura* gruel is cooking with milk. There is cow's milk in the *zariba* only, there is none in the village not even for pregnant or nursing women who have to content themselves with goat's milk or water.

Cow's milk is only for the wrestlers and the boys who will become wrestlers. In general the best food the Nuba have is given to the wrestlers: the very rare honey, for instance, is collected painstakingly and stored for the *kaduma*. The wrestlers are given the largest quantity of *dura*, peanuts and sesame, for all the Nuba of a village identify with their strong men. No one begrudges them their food since they all have the same wish for their sons and husbands to fight well in the traditional wrestling ceremonies.

Once the Nuba have breakfasted, two or three youths drive the cattle out of the kraal, playing their guitars at the same time. Before leaving the kraal the men sprinkle a few handfuls of ash on the back of each animal to protect it from bad luck. The remaining men now occupy themselves in their own fashion. While one group of young men paint stripes and patterns on one another's bodies, some lie on the pieces of round wood on which they have slept and play their instruments, and others lie lazily among the shrubs and begin to decorate themselves with bead necklaces. The young boys wash the calabashes and wooden spoons that they have made themselves, using only a little water, and hang them up to dry in the branches of the tree where they are also protected from the dust. This is also where they make most of their utility objects and decorative calabashes, fashioning them out of dried gourds and often burning complicated ornaments on them. They also make their guitars, sticks and shields here. Naturally they also have enough time for bodily decoration. This mainly consists of embellishing their heads by clever shaving, creating the most varied ornaments with imagination and patience. The Mesakin call these hair-styles *manga*. Most of the young men's ornamental scars are also made in the *zariba*. Then the men from the neighbouring *zariba* may pay a visit; everyone squats in the shade and there are long chats, much laughter and constant music. All this takes place with great composure. The movements of the Nuba are harmonious, there is no rush and everything radiates peace and quiet.

Meanwhile, the very young boys usually drive the cattle to the watering places. Every day the Nuba have to put a new coat of clay in the drinking troughs to prevent the water from seeping away. The water is drawn up from deep holes with calabashes and then poured into troughs through twigs which serve as filters. If a water hole dries up, men come from the *zariba* and dig deep holes in the ground until, if they are lucky, they hit muddy soil. Since they do not have shovels, they throw the mud up to the edge by hand until they have enough water to fill their clay pots. Since these water holes are often very deep, the men climb on each others' shoulders and form a pyramid. The heavy pot full of water is thrown up, caught, thrown up again and again, and then handed out of the water hole by the top man in the pyramid. This trick does not always work, for sometimes the heavy pot slips out of their hands, falls into the hole and breaks. But when this happens no one quarrels; the Nuba respond to such incidents only with laughter.

At sunset they all meet up in the *zariba* again. The fire is already burning, the *dura* gruel is boiling, and squatting or seated on stones they partake of their second meal of the day, which is the same as in the morning. Before going to sleep they shower themselves with the water stored in the calabashes and wash off the dust. While some Nuba sit round the fire making music, the others lie down on their 'beds'. These consist of five or six small round tree trunks laid next to one another. A stone serves as pillow and a small fire burns beween the individual 'beds' to warm the sleepers. This fire is constantly fanned and controlled by the boys who stand guard in turn at night. Unlike the Nuba in the villages, the *zariba* dwellers sleep in the open even in the strong, stormy winds. They love this life so much that they hate to give it up. This occurs when they abandon the life of a wrestler in order to assume the responsibilities of a father of a family, which usually happens at the ages of twenty-five to twenty-seven. But even family men come back to the *zariba* for a while.

Not all the young men who live in the *zariba* and take part in wrestling matches undergo the ceremony of initiation. Only youths who have distinguished themselves by above-average strength and skill during wrestling are chosen as heroes of their village community by this initiation. And it is only after initiation that a youth can take part in the matches between very strong wrestlers.

It is the father or the mother's brother who decides on this ceremony. The whole family saves up for a long time to clothe the young wrestler as splendidly as possible. They exchange *dura* or tobacco with Arab traders for yards of brightly coloured material which they cut in long strips and then wind round the torso of the youth. The ceremony takes place in the hut of the boy's father or uncle in the presence of only his family and best friends.

The ceremony is introduced with drum beats and the muffled sound of a horn. Then the father enters the hut with the red, green, white and blue strips of cloth over his arm and the ornamental hide in his hands. He is followed by his son, with lowered eyes. The hut gradually fills. A friend has placed a clay bowl full of white ash in front of the youth. The youth squats down and begins to rub the ash on his body. Another Nuba brings a large clay vessel in which is a white mash. The young man covers his head with this mash, mixed from milk beaten into cream and ash. Then he sits down on the ground, his legs spread out before him and remains in this position for a long time without moving. It looks as though he were meditating. The atmosphere affects all the people in the hut, and even the children no longer say a word. Only the drumming grows louder.

Suddenly the youth rises and raises his arms as a sign that the dressing can begin. While the father and one of his friends wind the wide, eleven-yard long strips of cloth round his upper body, the youth keeps his eyes almost shut. No change of expression betrays his feelings. An ornamental hide, decorated with cowrie shells, is attached to his arms, wrists and ankles, and finally a long necklace of beads is hung round his neck. His mother and brothers and sisters observe him proudly and with rapt attention. He no longer looks like a man of flesh and blood, but like a large exotic doll.

Once he is dressed his clothes are also dusted with ash. Suddenly the youth throws up his arms, emits muffled sounds and begins to dance with his hands. Then he bends over and takes up the initial stance of a wrestler. From the circle of those present a Nuba steps out to take up the youth's challenge to a wrestling match. There follows a display match in playful form which follows all the stages of a real match and in which the youth symbolically becomes the victor.

For every Nuba man selected for this ceremony, it signifies the highpoint of his life.

The Last of the Nuba

Captions for pictures on pages 105 to 128

105

This young kaduma *takes his position, as do most, quite seriously. The young men are responsible for ensuring their own strength by the pure life they lead in the cattle camp It is by being strong, and by victory in the wrestling ceremonies that they in turn ensure the continued mystical and physical strength of the people as a whole.*

106–107

At the first rays of the sun the wrestlers take their morning meal. While goats' milk is sometimes available in the village for pregnant women or infants, they are unlikely ever to have cow's milk. The only group privileged to drink cow's milk regularly is that of the kaduma *in the cattle camp, who eat millet boiled in milk as a gruel.*

108–109

Ash confers mystical strength and holiness on the man who wears it: it also protects cattle, and so a little is sprinkled on each animal as it is taken out of the camp in the early morning. The identification of man and beast is one complete and pervasive aspect of Mesakin religious belief. They share this with other pastoralist peoples like the Nuer who live to the south of them.

110–111

After the cattle leave the camp the wrestlers ash themselves over from head to foot. Weega is the name given by the Nuba to this ash, which plays such a large part in their life. They make it by burning the twigs of a certain bush. This snow-white ash has a double significance for them, one holy and the other practical. It bestows on them strength and good health, keeps the skin clean, protects them from insects and vermin and acts as body decoration.

112–113

Natu, Tadoro's champion wrestler, standing in the middle of the zariba. In front of him is the white ash next to the cooking place. (Every zariba is set up round a big, shady tree. The Nuba sleep in the open, and use tree trunks for bedsteads.) The small mud hut in the background is for the new-born calves.

114 above

The easy companionship of the cattle camp is something which men never forget. One's camp-mate remains in a special category of friend throughout one's life: he can demand and will show a comprehensive and enduring loyalty. Giving a friend a haircut in the camp is a small but typical way of showing this mutual trust and interdependence.

114 below

Particular friends, whose families are also close, will always choose to herd their animals in the same camp. Guri and Natu always shared their camp, and here they share their morning meal with another member of the zariba.

115

The basic purpose of wearing ash may be religious, but personal distinction is also sought in the decorative patterns in which it is applied. The additional decoration of white lines is made by applying butter-cream with the fingers.

116 above

The Nuba's morning toilet is finished. In keeping with their individuality, each has painted on a different 'suit'.

116 below

Now and again the men in the zariba go to visit their families. But they always come back at night to sleep in the zariba.

117

A young kaduma *from the Korongo Hills is setting off for a wrestling match some twenty miles away, carrying his spears and with his gourd slung around his waist.*

118–119

Young men who are living in the zariba will still, of course, visit their homes. But their clothing of ash demonstrates that they are really kaduma.

121

A young man who shows due seriousness of purpose and distinction as a wrestler, goes through a special initiation, generally conducted by his mother's brother. For Dia, today is his day. He is immersed in deep meditation.

122–123

The closest of the young man's comrades from the cattle camp will accompany him at the ceremony which takes place in his father's or his mother's brother's house. They will help him to prepare himself by applying the ash, and will give him psychological support at this important moment.

124–125

A sunbeam coming through the straw roof into the dark interior of the room increases the almost mystical atmosphere of the young man's clothing ceremony. The many lengths of coloured fabric wound round his body are the festive dress which he will wear from now on in his contests against the top wrestlers.

126–127

Concentration and intense seriousness characterise the young initiate's expression and demonstrate his consciousness of the significance of the occasion. He passes in spirit out of this world before re-entering it as a member of the superior wrestlers' class. An almost trance-like state intervenes between the two phases of his existence.

128

In front of this initiate's hut awaits a friend who will accompany him to the ceremony. On his arm he wears a leather armlet supporting the kind of small leather pouch which usually contains a charm. These are obtained from a local Kudjur.

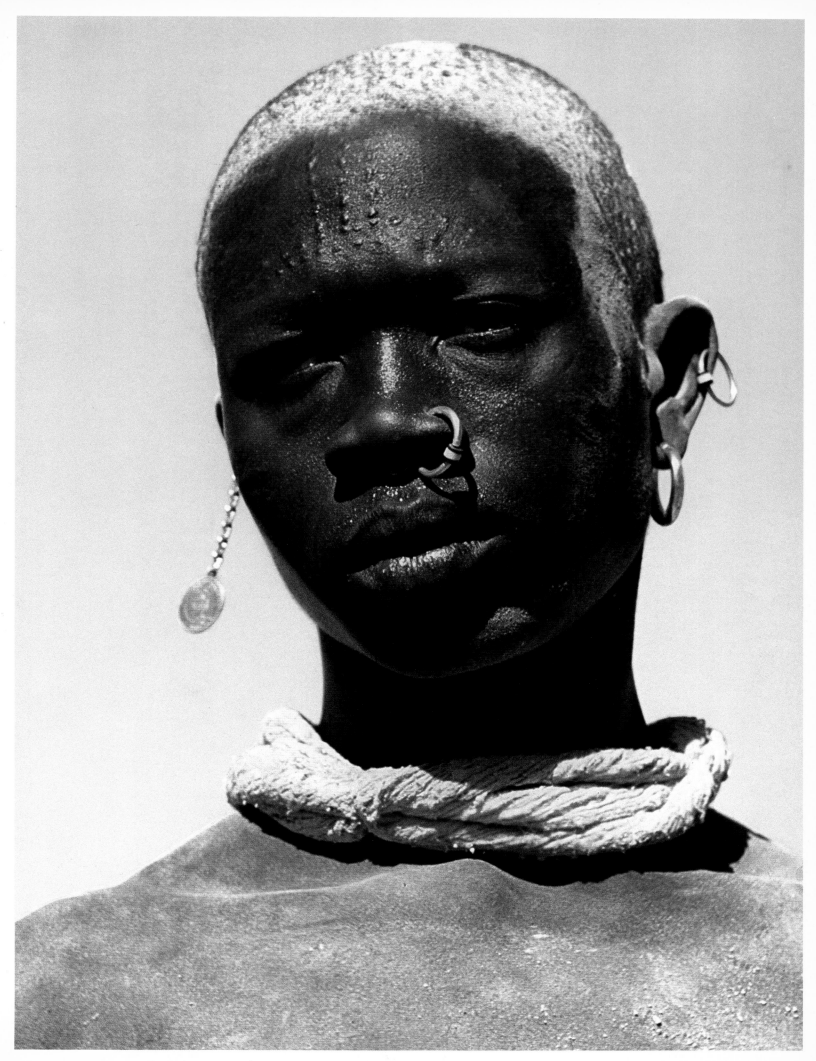

Chapter four

Wrestling

Those who have lived among the Mesakin soon learn that wrestling lies at the centre of their life. To a Nuba, wrestling far transcends the role of a sport: it is the expression of all that distinguishes the Nuba way of life. At a wrestling match the competitors wear ash and by this alone wrestling is seen to be a special activity.

Young children not yet able to walk properly begin to imitate the dancing and wrestling positions of their elders. From his earliest youth every healthy boy will prepare himself to become a wrestler. The children hold wrestling fêtes among themselves and decorate themselves in a similar way to their older brothers and sisters. The best of them rise to higher and higher grades. Their heart's desire is to be selected for 'initiation' by being the winner of the ceremonial wrestling matches, and then to be accepted into the highest grade of the strongest wrestlers.

As a rule it is the *Kudjur* and the council of elders who decide when and where a ceremonial wrestling match will take place. The wrestlers themselves and the rest of the community are not told until the last moment. All they know is that the ceremonial wrestling matches begin after the first *dura* harvest in November and December and last until the end of March. The frequency of the ceremony depends entirely on the harvest. In very good harvest years, matches can take place almost daily during these months. Three ceremonies can take place in a row in the same place. When harvests are poor and the *dura* yield scarcely suffices for subsistence, ceremonies are rare or do not take place at all.

As soon as the decision has been made, messengers are sent out to offer invitations wherever there are good wrestlers. Usually the messengers appear at sunset since this is when the Nuba return from working their fields. There are nearly always two messengers. One carries the *solodo*, a large, triangular leather cloth attached to a wooden stem which the Nuba always carry with them for cult matters. When he arrives at a village he slaps the ground several times. The same process takes place before the wrestlers enter the ring. While one messenger is slapping the ground with the *solodo*, the other blows a horn. Soon the Nuba crowd round the messengers and word of the invitation spreads quickly. Immediately boys

run to the remote *zariba* in order to pass on the joyful news to all the potential competitors. If the messengers come from distant places, for instance from the Korongo mountains, they spend the night with the Mesakin. Similarly the Mesakin messengers stay with the Korongo.

If the ceremony is to be a large one, with the most powerful wrestlers taking part, entire hill communities will attend, except for children and old people who cannot walk very far. If the site is far away they will arrange to arrive in the hosts' village the evening before the ceremony, and they will sleep in their hosts' houses. One such contest was between a number of Mesakin Nuba villages and several from the Korongo Hills. Following through the actual events of a contest, one can see how the complex symbolism of ash sums up for the Nuba a wide range of philosophical beliefs.

The first news of the forthcoming contest was announced to the people of Tutholo by the arrival of the heralds from Korongo. As usual, they were young men good at running, for they had a long way to travel to spread the invitation and challenge to many villages. One carried the trumpet which, like that of a mediaeval European herald, was both the symbol of his office and a necessary piece of his equipment. Blowing the trumpet and beating the ground to announce their arrival, the messengers spread their invitation-challenge; within a very few minutes there was no one in the village who did not know about the contest. Everyone was interested, and most of the people in the village accepted that as a matter of course they would all walk the twenty miles to watch the match.

Those most interested were naturally the *kaduma* who would fight. This was the moment for which they had prepared so long in the *zariba*, getting themselves into the right mental and physical state. The women prepared a lot of beer to take to Tokadindi, for they and other non-combatants could drink it, while the fighters are limited to water or milk. When the day arrived everyone set out early, for twenty miles is too far to walk during the heat of the day. Everyone was decorated in some way: with beads, ash, furs and calabashes which the wrestlers usually wear tied to their belt behind. The village flag, attached to a rod about sixteen to twenty-seven feet long, was carried at the head of the procession. Each village has a different flag which is kept in a

*Such is the importance attached
to wrestling among the Mesakin,
that children, almost as soon as
they can stand, begin to imitate
their elders whose positions and
actions they clearly observe. The
little boy in the present contest
went slightly beyond adult rules
in that, having been thrown by
the little girl – perhaps also in a
rather unorthodox manner – he
then, from the ground,
tripped her up.*

special house together with the ceremonial dress of the best wrestlers, the drum, the long horn and other wrestling requisites. It is in this house, or in front of it, that a champion wrestler is solemnly dressed and smeared with ash while his fellows watch. If the journey is so long that they have to rest overnight on the way, then the wives and sisters of the wrestlers carry the ceremonial dress in their baskets on their head. The women always form the rear of the procession, and their main burden is to bring the heavy pots with water and *marissa* to the ceremonies.

The Mesakin men have a great predilection for head-dresses, and here they show considerable imagination. The strongest wrestlers prefer old English topees which they decorate with long chains of beads that cover their face like a curtain. Others wear the red Turkish fez which their fathers or grandfathers won in battles with the Turks to the north in central Kordofan. Others again wear feathers, or head-dresses made out of pieces of cloth, feathers and old straw hats. They also attach objects of significance to their head-dresses, such as childrens' toys, dolls and even old picture frames which they have somehow come by.

On the way, the people from each village keep together as a group, generally led by their own champion wrestler who carries the village flag, and in front of each contingent their strongest wrestlers dance and recall past victories. The younger wrestlers, the married men and boys and the women carrying the gourds of *marissa* and water follow in a long line stretching back over the track. As they get closer to the wrestling-ground they close up to present a united and impressive spectacle to the villagers already arrived and who are waiting, scattered in the scanty bits of shade, for the wrestling to begin.

While waiting, the men who are to wrestle sit apart from the people who are less seriously involved. Conversation among them is quiet, tinged with anxiety that they should do well, conscious that the honour of their village depends on them, and aware of the essential seriousness of the occasion. The big special horn has been brought out of its special house for this important occasion, and its deep note sounds like the snorting of a bull in the characteristic rallying tone which victorious wrestlers will later imitate in their dances of triumph.

The size of the crowd grows as more and more villages arrive, until there are several thousand people assembled around their various flags. As each group of wrestlers move into the thickening crowd, the tension mounts.

Usually the matches begin in the early afternoon. But when established champions are fighting, they begin around midday. This is to show that the champions do not fear the heat and can even fight under a burning sun. As an external sign of their strength these champions wear a number of large 'tails' which they call *merre*. The more they wear of these 'tails' the more difficult it is to fight since they become very cumbersome. They are about two foot long and attached to a round, woven leather belt. Each ring has two 'tails' at the back, artfully put together from white or black goatskin. They are heavy and uncomfortable. The wrestlers put them on by climbing into the leather belt and then forcing it up above their hips. Some wrestlers wear up to eight of these *merre*. But this traditional wrestler's decoration is being worn less and less nowadays.

The time has come to begin. A group of five or six young men, covered in ash and painted with ornaments, run round the site. One of them carries the *solodo* which he slaps on the ground when the group pauses in its running. Other groups follow; a few minutes later the place is alive. Nuba stream in from all sides, carrying drums and wind instruments, the wrestler at their head. Near the wrestling ring they begin to dance. They stamp their feet, utter muffled sounds imitating the roar of a bull, (they call it *kaduma norzo*—the wrestlers' 'snort') and dance with their hands, or rather their fingers, moving them rapidly like large insects beating their wings. When the wrestlers approach the wrestling area in dense rows, dancing and roaring, the Nuba fall into a kind of ecstasy. At this stage the wrestlers are identified with the 'spirit' of their herds of cattle, and can no longer be addressed by their simple human name.

In one place several Nuba men have formed a circle. They crouch on their knees and put their foreheads to the ground. Behind them stand young men scattering ash from calabashes over the crouching group. Meanwhile the men hum in chorus while one of them calls out a word in solo, half singing, half shouting. This ceremony is a kind of prayer which the Mesakin call *tobbo*. It is meant to help their champion—in this case Natu from Todoro—to emerge as the victor. The long, twisted kudu horn is blown.

Then a large ring is formed in which a few of the less powerful wrestlers begin to fight. Several pairs can fight at the same time. The winner is he who throws his opponent down on his back. Unfair practice is forbidden, and each pair has a referee who decides to interrupt the fight when two wrestlers are equally strong and neither can throw the other. This kind of match counts as a draw.

Every strong wrestler has two assistants who usually live with him in the *zariba*: they are the young wrestlers. Before he begins to fight, he hands them his head-dress and his bead necklace which would encumber him during the match. One of these bead necklaces has a whistle attached to it, bought by barter from the Arabs, with which they announce their readiness to fight. The heavy brass arm bands are usually handed over too since they can injure an opponent. Nuba are never brutal when fighting, in fact the reverse. Wrestlers of equal strength, especially if they are friends, avoid a fight so that neither will humiliate the other by winning. And yet it is inevitable that injuries do occur. Particularly vulnerable are the ear lobes, which can catch and tear because of the silver earrings: sometimes they can even be pulled off. If this happens, or if the fighter bleeds from any other injury, the women immediately run up to him and lick the wound until it stops bleeding. A Nuba will show no sign of pain from his injuries.

Each wrestler can choose his opponent. Before they begin to wrestle, they take up the aggressive crouch and observe each other. Only at this point do they decide whether or not to fight each other. If the wrestler who has been challenged is not, for some reason, agreeable to the match, he rises and leaves, without saying a word. Perhaps it seemed to him that his partner was superior and he preferred to fight a less strong wrestler. But there are also challenges which no wrestler may refuse without losing face. If a wrestler wants a match with an opponent of high reputation, he will kneel down in front of him and, still in this attitude of humility, dance before him with his hands and arms, touching the ground with his palms. This challenge is always accepted and these are usually the most exciting matches because the wrestler challenged in this fashion does not want to lose under any circumstances.

Once they have paired off at the centre of each ring of spectators, three or four pairs of opponents gaze fixed at each other. For what seems an age, so great is the tension, the staring goes on, each fighter looking for a sign of indecision, seeking out weak spots. Then they begin to move, in quick, precise, assured movements. One stretches out a hand to his opponent's head, feeling, testing which way he will move; another circles warily; a third stands glaring, looking as immovable as a rock; another moves suddenly to one side in a feint designed momentarily to unbalance his opponent. Then the pairs move together heaving and straining, huge muscles bulging, until with a gasp and to a roar from the crowd, one throws the other to the ground. A particularly powerful wrestler sometimes lifts up his opponent like a sack and simply lays him on his back. The loser gets up quickly, disappointed but certainly not crushed. The victor is lifted shoulder high by the men from his village, and carried round the circle. He might then remain within the same circle, certainly if another member of his 'team' were fighting, or if there was a natural lull. Or the whole contingent might break away to join another ring and so repeat the process.

Meanwhile the first large ring has split up into several smaller rings in each of which a match is taking place. The respective communities set up their flag poles in each ring so that it is plain from afar in which ring the men of Tadoro, Tabala, Tamuri, or Tokadindi are currently fighting. The longer the matches last, the more impassioned and exciting they become and the noise at the site of battle becomes deafening. There is the constant beating of many drums, the cries of the spectators who are watching the matches with breathless suspense and accompany them, and the minute-long trills of the women's voices expressing their joy at the victory of a wrestler from their community. Some fights last only seconds, others several minutes. Often the fighting pair push their way through the circle of spectators. The referees carry twigs which they use as whips to clear them away. Often the spectators push in so close to the wrestlers as to impede their match, and then the referees move them back by beating their whip on the ground before, but never on, the spectators' feet.

It is difficult to say how often each wrestler will fight during such a ceremony since this varies. He may accept ten to

133

The Last of the Nuba

Captions for pictures on pages 137 to 168

137
A forthcoming wrestling contest is announced and the challenge issued by a 'herald', who runs round from village to village. He carries a 'trumpet', which, as with a mediaeval herald, is both his badge of office and a necessary piece of equipment for the job.

138–139
People will travel many miles to attend an important inter-village contest. A group of young men, travelling from Mesakin to Korongo on a journey of nearly twenty miles, rest in the scanty shade of a tree during the hottest part of the day.

140 above
A kaduma with his stick on the way to a wrestling match. His hair is dressed with a paste made from ash, and he wears some ash on his chest and arms—he will put on more when he arrives at the wrestling-ground as he prepares, with his team-mates, for the fight.

141
The originality of the dress adopted by distinguished wrestlers is considerable. Each wrestler chooses a different festival dress. This one has tied big fans of eagle's feathers on himself. Round his ankles he is wearing plongos, an ornament made from goat's hair and cowrie shells.

142–143
To tie a calabash to one's waist is a challenge to other wrestlers because it is an assertion that one cannot be thrown, since obviously that would break the gourd and make one's defeat uncomfortably obvious.

144–145
The contingent from each village is headed by the kaduma dressed in full wrestling paraphernalia and covered with ash. Women follow behind carrying calabashes of beer for non-combatants: the wrestlers drink only water during the match.

146 above
Three young men running to the tournament. They carry weapons which are sometimes used in other similar contests. The shield is of a traditional shape and is made from cowhide.

146 below
As the group of wrestlers lead their village contingent into the arena for the competition, they begin to dance. They lean forward and stamp their feet in an insistent and challenging rhythm which is designed to impress the opposition and to work up their own enthusiasm.

147 above
A member of the team trumpets through a kudu horn. The occasion is one on which special musical instruments, kept for the rest of the time in the special wrestling hut in the village, are brought out and used. This encourages the wrestlers, and makes a clear challenge to the other teams of wrestlers.

147 below
An important moment just before the team of wrestlers joins in the contest. The members crouch down on the ground while one of them intones an incantation asking the blessing of the ancestors. Another sprinkles them with ash.

148–149
The big horn is the pride of every hill community. It is made from the horn of a kudu antelope, which is lengthened with a mixture of clay earth and beeswax. Its hollow, primitive sound announces the start of the wrestling and spurs the wrestlers on.

150–151
The crowd which assembles for an important contest like the present comes from a considerable distance all round and can number many thousands. Each village rallies round its champion who bears its flag, and everyone is passionately concerned for the success and victory of their own team. After this contest spectators celebrate with much marissa consumed.

152
The concentration with which this young wrestler watches a bout shows the importance he attaches to understanding a possible opponent's technique.

152–153
A Korongo wrestler watches with great concentration as Natu (right), the champion wrestler of Tadoro (Masakin), fights a bout. The contests between the Korongo and the Masakin Nuba are the most exciting.

154–155
The watching girls are almost as emotionally involved as their men-folk in the successful outcome of the contest, but for them the occasion is more of a holiday. They do their bit for their village's prestige by looking their best and decorating themselves with care.

156–157
Natu is the champion wrestler in Tadoro and for some way around, and is therefore the leader of the village team. He carries the village 'standard' and wears a popular form of headdress: a solar topee decorated with strings of beads tied around the edge like a veil.

158 above
Nearly always several pairs fight simultaneously. This is the typical stance before an attack.

158 below
A small wrestling festival in Tamuri (Masakin), which lies hidden high up in the hills.

159 above
A victorious wrestler is carried out of the ring on his friend's shoulders. As an ornament he is wearing a Turkish fez adorned with cowrie shells, a legacy dating back to the end of the last century when his ancestors fought against the Turks.

159 below
In another bout, both contestants have attached calabashes to their waists. It is possible that both will manage to preserve them unbroken, for if a pair of wrestlers is so evenly matched that neither seems able to throw the other, the referee will eventually separate them and declare a draw.

160–161 above
The most prestigeous of the traditional wrestlers' ornaments is the merre. This is a belt of woven leather thongs, which ends in two long tails with goat's hair tufts. They are a considerable handicap, and to wear a number together offers one's opponent so much of an advantage that it is a thing which only a great champion, very sure of his own strength, would dare to do.

162
Other victors are hoisted onto the shoulders of their supporters and paraded around the ring cheered by the enthusiastic cries of their team-mates and of their fellow-villagers. They repeat the characteristic hand-movements of the victory 'dance.'

163 above
After a victory, the kaduma raises his voice and his hands in a paean of victory, which serves at once to advertise his success and to challenge other wrestlers.

163 bottom
The only tangible reward for victory is handed to a winner almost casually, but it is received with seriousness. It consists of a simple branch of acacia-wood. It will eventually be burnt in the cattle camp and part of the ash will be used to dress the wrestler for future matches. The other half of the ash will be kept and will accompany the wrestler, in the end, to his grave.

164–165
Children are as enthusiastic spectators of wrestling contests as their elders. If they find it difficult to see in the press of the crowd, they watch from a raised vantage point nearby.

166–167
The contests extend into the dusk. It is a profoundly religious occasion, drawing on the strength of the dead to revivify the living. The strength of the wrestlers vitalises the rest of the community, and will in due course pass to their successors who will hold similar contests in their honour.

168
Intensity of involvement is again the most characteristic and noticeable part of the expression on the face of this wrestler as he grasps his victor's branch.

Chapter five

Death

The Last of the Nuba

**Captions for pictures
on pages 177 to 200**

177
Natu was Napi's particularly close friend. They shared their cattle camp and had cemented the special relations of neggara—almost blood-brotherhood—by the exchange of favourite cattle. His expression, rather than the special funerary markings, shows the intensity of his grief.

178–179
The body is washed and laid out on a bed by the women of the family. Napi's mother seals the orifices of the head with wax. His grand-mother brings the seed rattles which he wore at wrestling matches, and which will accompany him in the grave. Napi's sister gives him his favourite knife.

180–181
A crowd of mourners waits for the cattle to arrive from which those to be sacrificed will be chosen. Ash here is a sign of mourning but its use emphasises the continuity of belief which runs through all the important Mesakin activities. It synthesises in one symbol harvesting, fertility, wrestling, the ancestors and death.

182–183
The cattle are assembled in the centre of the village, while the large crowd looks on. It is a sign of great respect to bring cattle for the dead—not all will actually be killed, but the gesture of friendship and concern has to be made. The family and the spirit of the dead will remember, and be grateful.

184–185
When the Nuba wear white mourning apparel it means that they were very close, either as relations or friends, to the deceased. The picture shows Nuba watching the ritual funeral ceremony.

186–187
The grief shown by the Nuba for their dead is genuine and deeply felt. Both men and women weep unrestrainedly.

188–189
The bier is carried down the hill. The generally stately progress is interrupted on the way by a period of lively dodging and weaving, by which the bearers ensure that they avoid the attentions of any malignant or interfering spirits who may be lurking in the path.

190 above
A successful wrestler burns his victory branches and carefully preserves the ash in horns. When the wrestler dies these horns represent the spirit of his past victories and his strength, and they are brought with ceremony to the funeral.

190 below
Part of the ash from the horns is scattered so that the dead man's closest friends may share his spirit. Just as the strength of the whole people was sustained by his victories in wrestling, so his spirit will continue to look after them when he has gone on.

191 above
The mourners are anxious to share in the ash—for to do so is to communicate directly with the spirit of the dead person. The ash in a mystical sense is the dead person, it is his finest essential part and through it his spirit will strengthen the survivors.

191 below
The horns are finally buried in their own separate grave, which will become the site of the wrestling matches held on the anniversary of this day to honour the dead man's spirit. The mourners try frantically to touch them for the last time—to embrace the dead man's spirit as he finally departs.

192–193
The only occasion when the Mesakin kill healthy cattle is when they are sacrificed at a funeral the sacrifice is performed by a kaduma noted for his purity and strength. The members of the dead person's clan may not eat the meat.

195
As long as the body remains above ground, guardians—painted perhaps like this to represent a skeleton—will stand at vantage points all round the village to ensure that any malignant spirits cannot pass to disturb the rest of the dead and the peace of the community.

196–197
The closest relatives of the dead man spend the night in the fields near the grave, lamenting in song and weeping his departure.

198–199
Most of the mourners at the funeral wait silently till dusk when all is over. While the closest relations spend the night in vigil, the rest slip silently away in the darkness.

200
The grave is covered with stones and a pile of earth. Spears, calabashes and pots are broken and placed on the grave—they, like him, are dead. A protection of thorns prevents disturbance of the tomb by predatory animals and ensures that the dead will rest in peace.

202–203
The Mesakin Nuba cover themselves with ash for all important social and religious occasions. Ash demonstrates, for the onlookers, the seriousness of the wearer's intentions, concentrates his own mind on the spiritual aspects of the ceremony and mystically increases his strength.

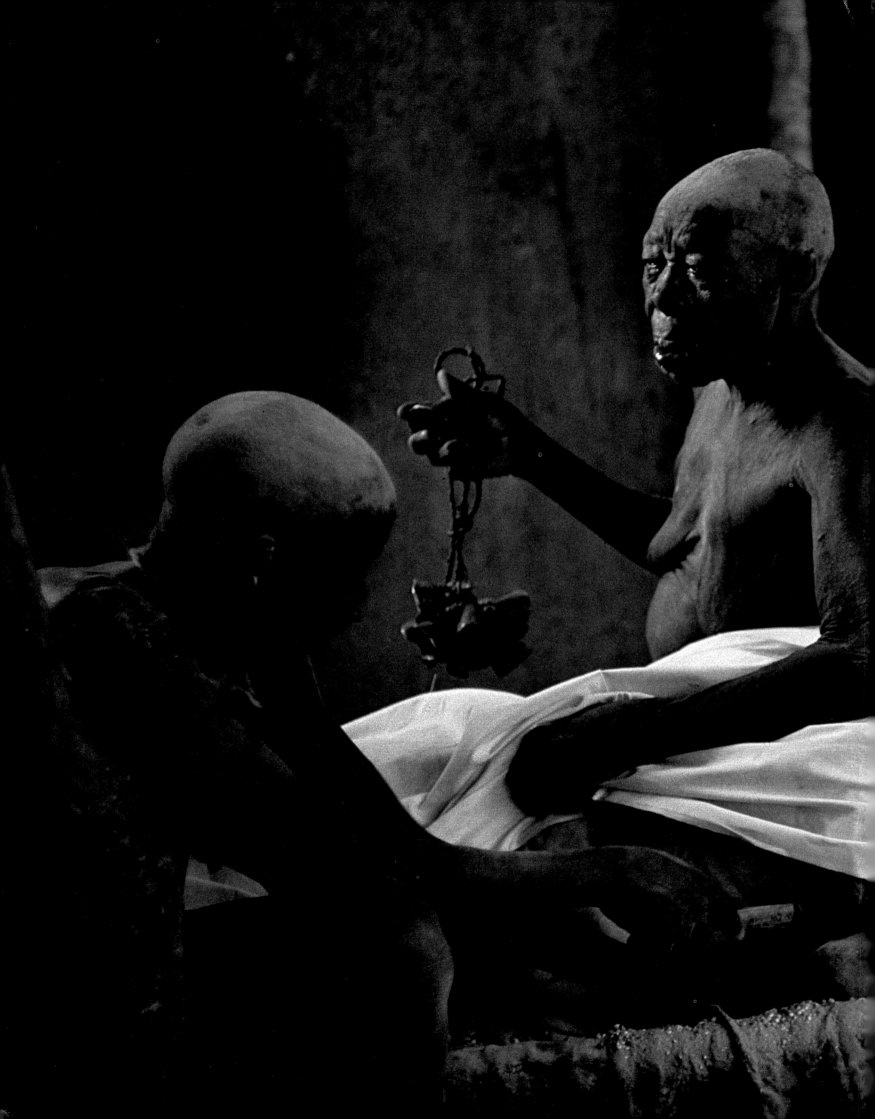

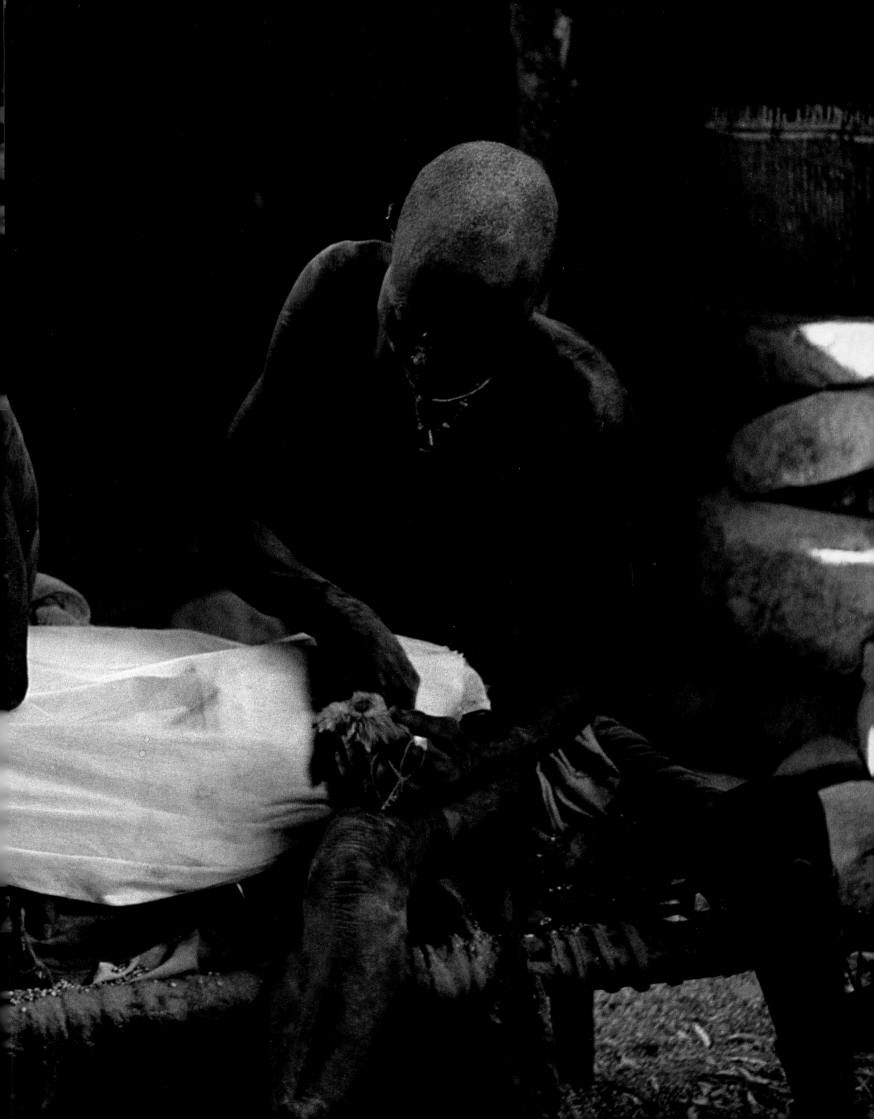

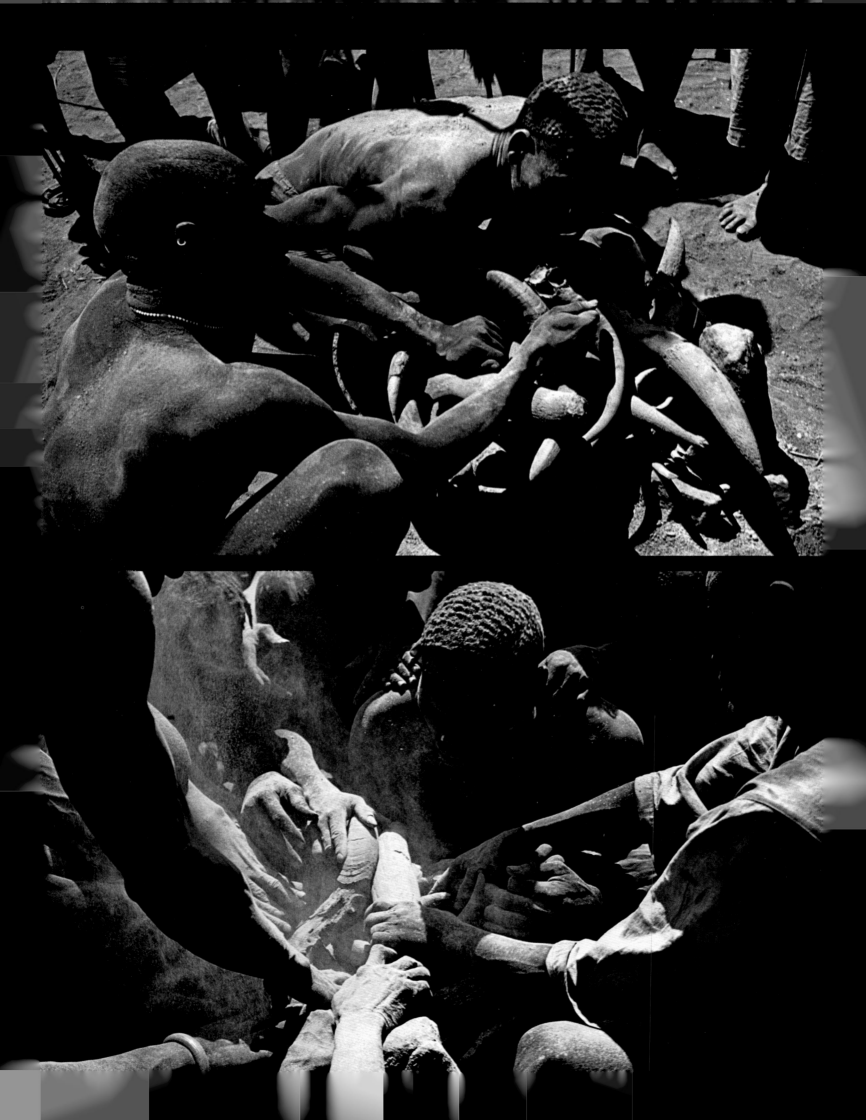

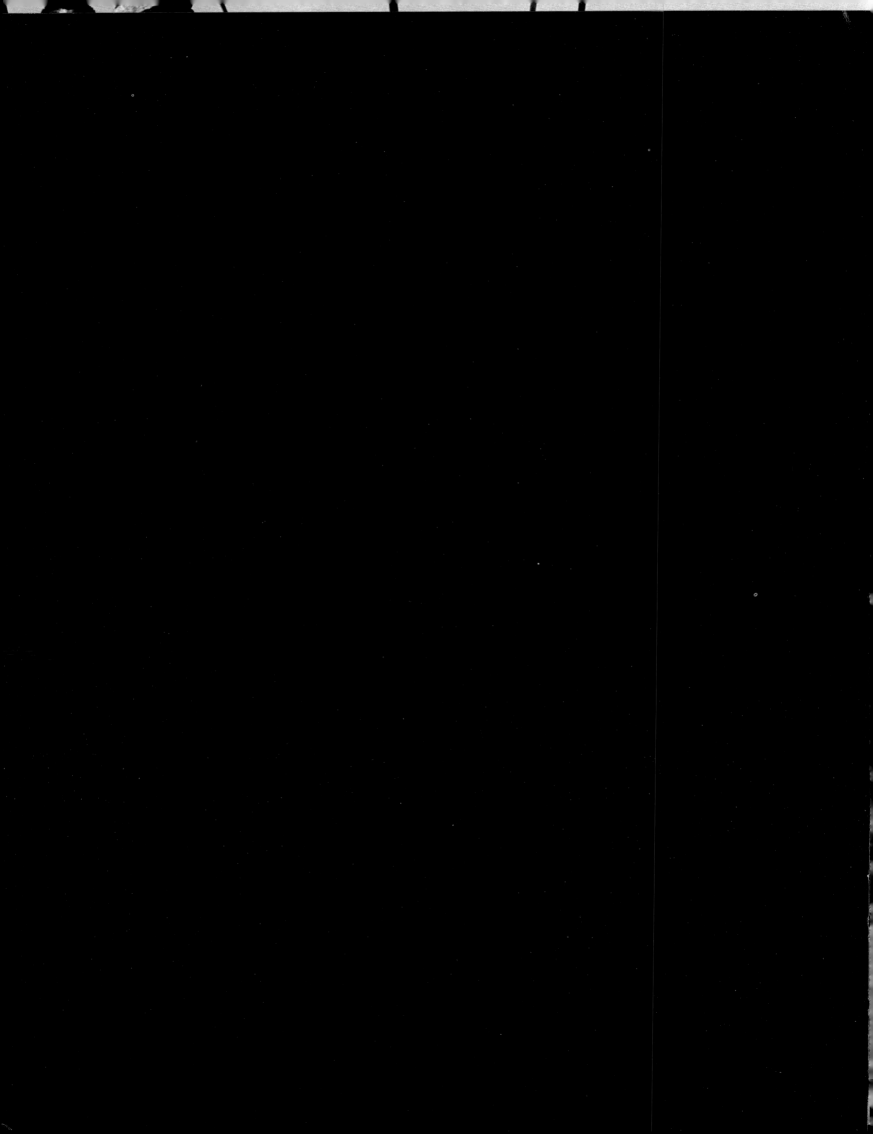

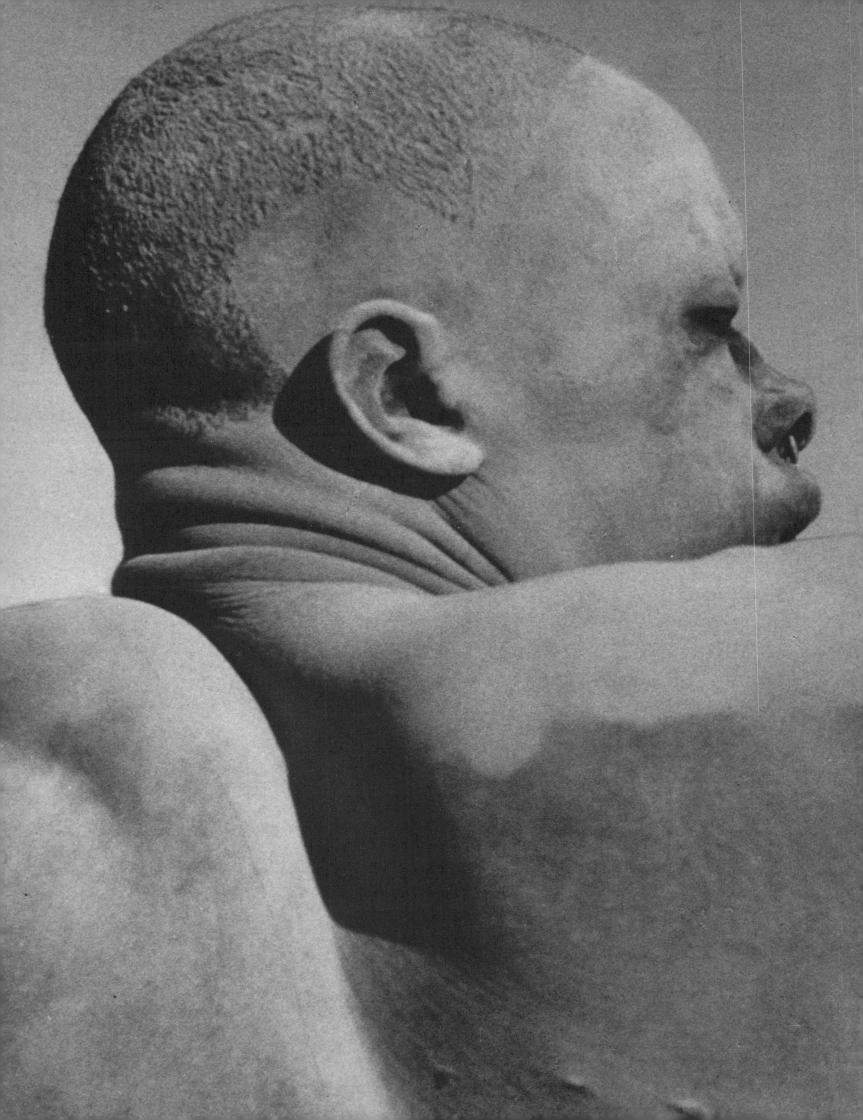

FURTHER READING LIST

With the exception of queries answered by Rolf Engel about agriculture,
the author did not refer to the following recommended reading list.

S.N.R. *Sudan Notes and Records (including Proceedings of the Sudan Philosophical Society)*
J.R.A.I. *Journal of the Royal Anthropological Institute*

ARKELLA, A. J. *A History of the Sudan to 1821* London 1962

BARBOUR, K. M. *Peasant Agriculture in the A-E Sudan* (Cyclost.) Khartoum 1953

BEER, C. W. *The Manufacture of Nuba Stone Knob Sticks* S.N.R. XVIII, 1935, ii, 294

BELL, G. *Nuba Fertility Stones* S.N.R. XIX, 1936, ii, 313

BELL, G. W. *Nuba Agricultural Methods and Beliefs* S.N.R. XXI, 1938, ii, 237

BOCK, F. *Zu den neuen Sprachen von Süd-Kordofan* Zeitschr. für Kolonialsprachen III, 1912–13

BOLTON, A. R. C. *The Dubab and Nuba of Jebel Daier* S.N.R. XIX, 1936, i, 93

CORKILL, N. L. *A Kadugli Cobra Trap* S.N.R. XVIII, 1935, i, 131

CORKILL, N. L. *The Kambala and other Nuba Festivals* S.N.R. XXII, 1939, ii, 205

ELLES, R. J. *The Kingdom of Tegali* S.N.R. XVIII, 1935, i, 1

ENGEL, R. *Spezielle Untersuchungen der Landwirtschaft in den Nubabergen* Max-Planck Gesellschaft Institut München 1964

FARIS, J. *Nuba Body Painting* London 1972

FLETCHER, C. A. *The Dilling Ceremony* S.N.R. VI, 1923, i, 31

FROBENIUS, L. *Und Afrika sprach* 1913, 3 Band, 4 Kapitel Vita Deutsches Verlagshaus Berlin-Ch.

HASSAN, Y. F. *Penetration of Islam in the Eastern Sudan* S.N.R. XLIV, 1963, 1

HAWKESWORTH, D. *The Nuba Proper of Southern Kordofan* S.N.R. XV, 1932, ii, 159

HENDERSON, K. D. D. *Fung Origins* S.N.R. XVIII, 1935, i, 149

HENDERSON, K. D. D. *Nubia and Nuba* S.N.R. XVIII, 1935, ii, 325

HENDERSON, K. D. D. *Nubian Origins* S.N.R. XXI, 1938, i, 222

HILLELSON, S. *Nubian Origins* S.N.R. XIII, 1930, i, 137

KAUCZOR, P. D. *The Afitti Nuba of Jebel Daier* S.N.R. VI, 1923, 1

KINGDON, F. D. *Throwing Knives among the Nuba* S.N.R. XIX, 1936, i, 190

KINGDON, F. D. *Bracelet Fighting in the Nuba Mountains* S.N.R. XXI, 1938, i, 197

LUZ, O. *Proud Primitives the Nuba People* 1966, National Geographic Vol. 130, No. 5

MacDIARMID, D. N. *Notes on Nuba Customs and Languages* S.N.R. X, 1925

MacDIARMID, P. A. & D. N. *The Languages of the Nuba Mountains* S.N.R. XIV, 1931, ii, 149

MacMICHAEL, H. A. *A History of the Arabs in the Sudan* Cambridge 1922

MEINHOF, C. *Eine Studienfahrt nach Kordofan* Abhandlungen des Hamburgischen Kolonialinstituts XXXV, 1916

NADEL, S. F. *The Hill Tribes of Kadero* S.N.R. XXV, 1942, i, 37

NADEL, S. F. *The Nuba* London 1947 For Mesakin and Korongo see especially Chapter VIII, p. 267

NADEL, S. F. *Two Nuba Religions: an essay in comparison* American Anthropologist 57 (4), 1955, 661

NALDER, L. F *Throwing Knives in the Sudan* S.N.R. XVIII, 1935, ii, 297

RODGER, G. *Le village des Nubas* Paris 1955

ROTHE, F. K. *Family Background and Schooling* 1969, Georg Westermann-Verlag, Band 6

SAGAR, J. *Notes on the History, Religion and Customs of the Nuba* S.N.R. V, 1922, 173

SELIGMAN, B. Z. *Note on the Language of the Nubas of Southern Kordofan* Zeitschr. für Kolonialsprachen I, 1910–11

SELIGMAN, C. G. *The Physical Characters of the Nuba of Kordofan* J.R.A.I. XL, 1910

SELIGMAN, C. G. & B. Z. *Pagan Tribes of the Nilotic Sudan* London 1932, 366–412

STRUCK, B. *Somatische Typen und Sprachgruppen in Kordofan* Zeitschr. für Äthiopien LII, 1920–21

STEVENSON, R. C. *The Nyamang of the Nuba Mountains of Kordofan* S.N.R. XXIII, 1940, i, 75

STEVENSON, R. C. *Linguistic Research in the Nuba Mountains I* S.N.R. XLIII, 1962, 118

STEVENSON, R. C. *Some aspects of the spread of Islam in the Nuba Mountains* S.N.R. XLIV, 1963, 9

STEVENSON, R. C. *Linguistic Research in the Nuba Mountains II* S.N.R. XLV, 1964, 79

SWEENEY, C. *Jebels by Moonlight* London 1969

G. W. T. *Nuba Houses (note)* S.N.R. XIV, 1931, ii, 196

TOTHILL, J. D. (ed) *Agriculture in the Sudan* London, 1948, 831ff

TUCKER, A. W. & MYERS, C. S. *A Contribution to the Anthropology of the Sudan* J.R.A.I. XL, 1910

The author was so fascinated by this photograph, taken by the famous English photographer George Rodger, that for years she tried to find the Nuba in order to study the life of these primitive people. (Photo: George Rodger)

The Nuba of the Kordofan in the Sudan – specifically the Mesakin and Korongo Nuba – are perhaps the most remarkable tribal group in Africa to have survived the enormous changes which have overcome the rest of the Continent. Well away from trade routes, remote in the arid mountains of the central Sudan from the disruptions of alien cultures and the meretricious ideas of Western man, these fragile groups of noble men have clung to their traditional culture with a rare and stubborn devotion, which has so far preserved them from the Arabization of so many of the people of that vast, but sparsely inhabited, area.

Over a period of ten years, Leni Riefenstahl has lived on and off with the Mesakin Nuba, sometimes for several months at a time. Here she presents her remarkable record of the everyday rhythms of life; of eating, sleeping, building, gathering food and taking their leisure; of the great cycles of birth, marriage and death; and of the remarkable central factor of their culture and religion: the wrestling contest.

It is, alas, a commonplace to represent a tribal group, whose life has evolved in an inspired and intimate harmony with their environment, as being on the brink of extinction. For all their physical magnificence, the Mesakin Nuba are indeed a fragile stem of the human race. But there will be perhaps no people in the world doomed to extinction as an ethnic entity who will have been survived, for so long as *our* civilization lasts, by a more devoted record such as Leni Riefenstahl has brought out from Africa.

power in 1933, commissioned Riefenstahl to make a documentary on the Nuremberg Rally in 1934.

Riefenstahl's refusal to submit to Goebbels' attempt to subject her visualisation to his strictly propagandist requirements led to a battle of wills which came to a head when Riefenstahl made her film of the 1936 Olympic Games, *Olympia*. This, Goebbels attempted to destroy; and it was only saved by the personal intervention of Hitler.

With two of the most remarkable documentaries of the 1930's to her credit, Riefenstahl continued making films of her devising, unconnected with the rise of Nazi Germany, until 1941, when war conditions made it impossible to continue.

Her acquaintance with the Nazi leadership led to her arrest at the end of the Second World War: she was tried twice, and acquitted twice. Her reputation was in eclipse, and she was half forgotten – although to a whole generation of Germans her name had been a household word.

During the 1950's she turned from moving pictures to photography, in which she soon began to excel through her unique vision and perfectionism. In the noble tribesmen of the arid areas of eastern and north-eastern Africa she found subjects ideally suited to her temperamental needs and artistic skills. Her work as an observer and chronicler of the Mesakin Nuba of the Kordofan is the crowning glory of her photographic achievement.

Coinciding with the publication of this work has come the rehabilitation of Riefenstahl's reputation both as a film maker and photographer. In her seventieth year, the London *Sunday Times* commissioned her to cover the 1972 Munich Olympic Games. Simultaneously, her early films have been revived in film societies throughout the world.

Still constantly traveling, Leni Riefenstahl's headquarters are in Munich.